# Remember the
# Sweet Things

1999

504

# Remember the Sweet Things

*One List, Two Lives,
and Twenty Years of Marriage*

Ellen Greene

*wm*

WILLIAM MORROW

*An Imprint of* HarperCollins*Publishers*

HarperCollins books may be purchased for educational, business, or sales promotional use. For information please write: Special Markets Department, HarperCollins Publishers, 10 East 53rd Street, New York, NY 10022.

FIRST EDITION

*Designed by Nicola Ferguson*

Library of Congress Cataloging-in-Publication Data has been applied for.

ISBN 978-0-06-147924-3

09 10 11 12 13   OV/RRD   10 9 8 7 6 5 4 3 2 1

*for Marsh*

# Contents

# Introduction

FOR TWENTY-ONE YEARS I KEPT A RUNNING LIST of funny, thoughtful things my partner, Marsh, said and did. Not especially hilarious or saintly things, just nice guy/good husband stuff. Take something mundane, like his working late on a Friday night to build me a kitchen shelf. Seen as the act of a tired man who didn't enjoy two-by-four carpentry, it made the list. If he whistled while he worked, he earned double mention for his great attitude.

I would jot things down surreptitiously, usually soon after they happened. Sometimes fistfuls of paper scraps would pile up in my purse before I had a chance to re-write them on the master list. A year's worth of entries filled six or seven handwritten 8½ × 11 sheets. I write small, so that was more than one hundred entries every year. For Valentine's Day, I made copies, put them in a card, and gave them to Marsh.

His reaction was invariably the same. He would open the card, smile at finding the pages inside, and count them. "*Yet again* I have apparently been an exemplary spouse," he would say. Smiling, he would sit down in his comfortable green chair and start to read.

I would fake being busy in another room. After a few minutes, I'd hear sniffling and know he was crying. He would finish reading, come and find me, rock me in his arms, give me a long, serious kiss, and say, "Thank you, El." Just that, no more. For me, the response was perfect. Being appreciated for appreciating him—what could be more basic?

The basics came more easily to me this time around in my life. Divorce had taught me some things, if only that the pain of another split might do me in. Plus, my children, Jennifer, age sixteen, and Michael, age fourteen, deserved better. After the acrimonious ending of our marriage, their father had left the United States, remarried, and become a hurtful nonpresence in their lives. They continued to be understanding and forgiving of me, accepting and affectionate toward Marsh, their new stepfather. I told myself that if I blew it with this man who treated me and them so lovingly, I was a fool and they had a loser for a mother.

The list idea had occurred to me early in our relationship. But remembering all the endearing moments wasn't what I had in mind. I'd been all too good at that with previous partners. I had stayed too long with men who treated me poorly. Too often I chose to remember the occasional act of kindness while conveniently forgetting the more typical lack of caring, especially where my kids were concerned.

This selective memory of mine had come to hurt me and hurt my children. I couldn't let it control our lives again. I was wildly in love with Marshall Whitney Greene and had zero objectivity about him. I decided to force myself to write down, as they happened, any hurtful thing he said or did, all excuses and rationalizations aside. The smallest of psychic wounds inflicted on me or Jennifer or Michael would be duly transcribed. Later, when this relationship headed south, as experience had taught me was inevitable, I would force myself to read all the ugly little entries. I would see him for the man he truly was, and it would feel easier to cut my losses sooner rather than later.

But Marsh didn't give me any material to work with. After four months of dating, I didn't have a single line item. Month after month, he continued to be his same old considerate, quick-witted, gentlemanly self. There was so little tension between him and my teenagers, it almost made me anxious. Was this some kind of act the three of them could never expect to keep up? But they really seemed to like each other, and Marsh made time for them without any prompting from me. He invited them to go skiing with him one Saturday. He took them out to dinner one night when I was out of town on business. "I enjoyed helping you with your math homework," he said to Michael. "I'm looking forward to attending your band concert," he remarked to Jennifer. We believed him.

So I changed tactics. Maybe my initial love-struck take on Marsh had been dead on, and indeed he was The Man of My Dreams. If so, why create a self-fulfilling prophecy by concentrating on the negatives? Why not turn this list-making strategy on its head and instead write down the positives? Instead of relying on selective memory this time, I decided to create proof that this love of ours had legs. Yes, tough times might be inevitable. But I could contrast their number with a written record of the good times, and this record would help me stay the course.

And so was born the new list I came to call "Remember the Sweet Things." It's laughable now, to think of my ever having needed to relive the past in order to endure the present with Marsh. He gave me fresh material every year, with few repeats, even though some of his familiar lines always made me smile. Granted, I stretched the definition of what qualified as a sweet thing to include memorable experiences we shared. Still, one hundred ten pages of sharing, kindness, humor, and affection make for a nice love story.

# Chapter 1

## *Meeting Marsh:*
## *1983, 1984*

I KNEW BETTER THAN TO ANSWER A BLIND AD IN the Help Wanteds. If the employer won't tell you who they are, chances are they're hiding something from their own people. Or so we Human Resource types often counseled others. But I was desperate, so I sent in my résumé.

It had been a disastrous six months since moving from Colorado to Massachusetts. An experienced job skills trainer, I couldn't find a job to even apply for, the labor market was so tight. Both of my kids detested their new schools in Springfield. And my relationship with Joe, the reason we came to the East Coast in the first place, had begun to unravel almost upon arrival. So when someone named "Mosh Green" from "Wista, Mass" called, I jumped at the chance to interview with him. It was for a training manager's job at Jamesbury

Corporation, a small valve manufacturing company an hour away. I didn't know exactly what a valve was, but what difference could it make? I thought. They were looking for management development; I had written and taught management skills programs for corporate giants like GTE and Mobil. I didn't know where Wista was, either, but based on directions from Mosh and a look at a map, I figured it had to be Worcester. I pictured Mosh as a short, balding, Jewish guy.

Road conditions were bad the day of the interview, with the highway from Springfield to Worcester iced over and visibility down to 50 percent. I drove through a snowstorm for almost two hours and arrived edgy and late. "Mosh" turned out to be Marsh, short for Marshall, and he was jumpy, too.

"We have to make it fast," he said, his left leg doing a jig to a beat of its own. "I need to make a presentation to the executive committee in twenty minutes."

During the course of the next five minutes, Marsh kept glancing at his watch and eyeing the stack of note cards in front of him. He asked stock questions like "Tell me about yourself" and "What's your ideal job?" At least he was too distracted to notice that I was staring at him. Bluer eyes, a better haircut, and he could pass for Paul Newman. Even the crinkly-eyed smile was similar. And Marsh Greene was taller—all the better. Six feet, I guessed, and probably in his early fifties. And how about the Brahmin accent; how charming was that? I was almost enjoying myself.

But it's tough to sell yourself to someone barely paying attention. After ten minutes, I put him out of his misery.

"I really think I'd be a good fit for this job, and I'm not sure there's time now for me to tell you why," I said, pulling the words out of an interviewing skills course I had once taught. "Could we reschedule this interview at a time better for you?"

Marsh looked down at his shoes, grinned, and agreed that another time would be better. He apologized for my having to make two long, hazardous drives, asked if the next afternoon would work for me, and suggested splitting the driving distance by meeting at a halfway point.

"Just in case the weather doesn't break," he said.

I am not prescient. But if I had been able to see myself as the future Ellen Greene, the Sweet Things list could have begun then and there.

He suggested meeting at the Publick House in Sturbridge, Massachusetts, because he would be joining a group for dinner there later that evening. Located on the old Boston Post Road, the inn dated back to the 1700s. It was a beauty—a classic white saltbox with black shutters. I arrived half an hour early, just to play it safe, and gave myself a tour. Standing there in the middle of a scene from early American history, I felt almost reverential.

We met in the dining room and faced each other over a wide plank table. Marsh had his back to a low-burning fire and was framed by the stone fireplace. Over a late lunch, he talked at length about Jamesbury and its product line of industrial valves. *Oh my God, could I have picked a more tedious product than valves,* I thought. The topic and the fire were making me drowsy.

He moved on to explain more about the job I'd applied for. I'd be working with him on a performance improvement program for the company's twelve hundred employees. I'd also be training all the managers and supervisors on how to be better bosses. *Great*, I thought. *I get to be the know-it-all newcomer telling everyone how to do their jobs.*

I asked him about himself. He alluded vaguely to a career in manufacturing management. He'd set up a factory in Spain, worked for a small envelope company, and now had four years in at Jamesbury.

"Are you a native New Englander?" I asked. As if no one else in the United States could pronounce their *r*s either.

"Yes, my family arrived from England in 1636," he said, "but I descended from unadventurous stock. In over three hundred years, we've only made it fifty miles inland to Worcester."

My first Olde Yankee, I thought, handing me a well-rehearsed line.

But mostly I thought this job in a small manufacturing company would make a nice resting place. I was exhausted after two poor career choices, one in telecommunications, the other in Big Oil. During the last five years, my kids and I had moved three times to three different states. And now, after staying way too long in a troubled personal relationship, I was pulling the plug on it, just as I had done with my marriage to Carlos ten years before.

Carlos and I had met in Costa Rica in 1968. For me, going to Costa Rica by myself was a gutsy move. I had grown up in a working-class home in Fond du Lac, Wisconsin, a town of thirty-five thousand surrounded by small family dairy farms. In my eighteen years at home, I had traveled out of state exactly once, when a caravan of proud family members drove to New York for my older brother's graduation from West Point. I went to all-white Catholic schools for twelve years and had to ask for a dispensation from our pastor, Monsignor Riordan, to attend my own state university at Madison. For midwestern Catholics, it was the heralded "den of godless Communism," where parents and priests feared for our losing "The Faith."

At Madison, I was a poor excuse for a Spanish major who couldn't work up the nerve in class to speak the language. When I did come out with something, I sounded like a shy tourist reciting memorized phrases from a guidebook. My self-help plan was to spend a summer working in a Spanish-speaking country. I could afford a ticket as far south as Panama. My mother disapproved of this plan, but I was on my own, paying my own way through school; therefore, I felt entitled to disregard her opinion.

To be honest, I would disapprove, too, if my daughter landed a job in a foreign country the way I did. I bleached my hair blond, took a photo of the new me, and made copies. I slipped a photo into a letter handwritten on bright blue stationery and sprayed it all with Ambush perfume. A book in the UW Business School library gave me the addresses of Central American branches of U.S. companies, and I sent off a batch of one hundred odorous letters in which I begged for a job, any job.

Incredibly, within a few months of the mass mailing, six offers had come in. One from the Manhattan Shirt Company sounded the most promising. The CEO had graduated from a U.S. university, and my letter reminded him, he said, "of those playful days." He not only offered me an office job I thought I could handle in Spanish but also a room in the house of his secretary's aunt.

He was playful, all right. The secretary turned out to be his mistress. And in my one time alone with him in his office, he of the potbelly and Pancho Villa mustache chased me around his desk like a scene from some kind of bad burlesque sketch. But Carlos was already on the scene and came to my rescue.

Carlos and I had met a month earlier on a Sunday afternoon, at the weekly Costa Rica Country Club dance. A "meat market" masquerading as a cotillion, this dance was purported to be the guaranteed place for twentysomethings of the better set to dress up and meet. Ambitious up-and-comers like Carlos also finagled their way in, and all young foreigners, especially women, could count on an eager reception. My second week in the country, the niece of my landlady invited me to the Sunday affair. Within minutes of our walking in the door, a tall Latino with the brooding dark eyes of legend approached me, introduced himself as Carlos "El Pana" (Carlos the Panamanian), and asked me to dance. He was an excellent dancer, and I could barely follow his lead, which flustered me. But he just laughed and persisted in teaching me the cumbia and the rumba, as he monopolized that evening and most others for the next month. I was delighted.

Now Carlos helped me find another job, and a more interesting one, as an overseas telephone operator at the Costa Rican national phone company. At night after work, he took me dancing and to the movies. We zipped around town on his Vespa, stopping at open-air eateries for barbacoa served with soft corn tortillas fresh from the griddle. Or we'd meet his friends at hole-in-the-wall bars for setups of cheap rum and Coke, with free snacks of fried plantains and ceviche to keep us there drinking. As the long-legged gringa, I was the catch of the day, the central attraction. Both of us lapped up the attention.

Two months after meeting him, Carlos appeared under my boardinghouse window at midnight. He brought along flowers and two guitar players, who sang about my beautiful green eyes. This didn't happen much in Wisconsin. I called my parents.

"I'm in love, I'm not coming home in September, and I'm transferring to the Universidad de Costa Rica," I told them, making sure to trill the r in Rica. My mother told me later she thought I was probably pregnant and hiding out, waiting to deliver my baby, conceived back in godless Madison.

I wasn't pregnant, but I was in love, and I sure did want to marry Carlos. This was 1968. The birth control pill had only just become available. My Zoology 101 professor's much-talked-about final lecture of the semester compared the various methods of birth control and drew a standing-room-only crowd of a thousand students, all hanging on his every word. Fear of pregnancy and horrific abortion stories dominated our conversations and lives as coeds. And, in my case, it resulted in a debilitating level of inexperience. At least technically a virgin when I met Carlos, I had no one to compare him to when we "went all the way." Worse yet, I equated marriage with permission for sex: If we were going to "do it," we should be married. Carlos might even have agreed in theory; he was, after all, a cradle Catholic educated by Dominican brothers.

In any event, he acquiesced to the considerable pressure I began to put on him to commit to me. We were married the next summer in St. Joseph's, my home church in Fond du Lac. I borrowed my cousin Barbara's wedding dress and made myself a veil from some Spanish lace I found in a backstreet shop in San José. I hadn't wanted a big church wedding, but it meant a lot to my mother, so we went along with the sit-down dinner, champagne toasts, and multitiered cake she was happy to arrange to her own specifications.

Within three years, Carlos and I had ourselves two little ticos, Jennifer and Michael, both born in the Clinica Católica in San José. I finished a teaching degree in English as a Second Language and got a job in a new bilingual school. We bought a used Volkswagen van so Carlos could start a small tour business, running tourists up to volcanoes and out to coffee plantations.

But we were not the happy young couple in their struggling years, at home after a busy day of building a future together for our little family. We rarely saw each other. In year two of our marriage, Carlos took on some bookkeeping clients whom he claimed he could only see in the evening. A couple of clients and a couple of nights ratcheted up to four clients and four nights, until finally he was out most nights of the week and not home by the time I fell into bed, exhausted from teaching and taking care of our babies.

I screamed at him as he headed for the front door: Where are you going? Why does it have to be tonight? Who are you seeing? In Spanish. In English. In letters left on the dining room table for him to read after I was asleep, I wailed in protest and pleaded with him to spend more time with his family. More of the same in the morning: Where did you go? What took you so long? Who were you with?

Sometimes Carlos tried to placate me with short, vague answers. Most of the time he blew me off with a "not now" or "we'll talk later." If especially annoyed at my anger, he riveted expressionless eyes on me and stared me down. "Me hizo comer hielo," they say in Spanish. "He made me eat ice." Finally, after a bitter year of rage and silence, he revealed himself. "I owe you no explanations," he said. "I am the man of the house. You are my wife and the mother of our children."

What the hell did that mean? Had I married some macho stereotype? Who expected me to act like the stereotype's counterpart—a passive, long-suffering female partner who would tolerate whatever bad behavior he chose to dish out? Apparently, the answer was yes. How naive and ignorant both of us had been. How little we had known each other before we married, and how wide the cultural divide we each now had to cross.

Not that this should have come as a big surprise. I knew that Carlos was the illegitimate son of Julia, a Nicaraguan curandera (folk healer), and Jorge Abdullah, a Turkish merchant. That he had been conceived while they lived together on a Standard Fruit plantation. That Julia had chopped off the tip of Jorge's ear with a machete, after chasing him out of the bed he shared with another woman, and before she ran him off, never again to be a part of Carlos's life. That she had shipped Carlos out of their one-hitching-post jungle town on the Panamanian border at age eleven, to board with a family in San José so he could attend high school. I had slept in Julia's house and witnessed her indifference to her son and grandchildren; her story is a book in itself. With such a background, where would Carlos have learned to be the caring husband and family man I now demanded?

I saw a return to the U.S. as our best hope for saving our marriage. Naive as ever, I thought that a combination of removal of "occasions of sin" (Catholic for "temptation") and exposure to good role models (the men in my family) would turn Carlos around. Plus I was lonely and homesick. Living in the States would mean a drastic change for him, but an enviable adventure that he could brag about as well. He agreed, and in 1972 we moved to Colorado. I landed a job at Fort Carson teaching English to mostly Puerto Rican G.I.s returning from Vietnam. Carlos, excited but nervous to be out of Central America for the first time, agreed to stay home with the kids while he accustomed himself to life in the U.S. Boredom set in quickly, however, and he went to work painting houses.

We had kidded ourselves about the depth of the chasm that separated us and strained our relationship. Physically, we were sharing the same space most evenings now, but mentally, we had retreated to our own solitary corners. If we talked at all, it concerned the kids or logistics. Control remained our big issue—who had it, how it was wielded. For example, I managed our finances, but I could never be sure of the amount of money I had to work with. I knew how much Carlos charged for a paint job, plus when he started and finished. But what he gave me each week depended on his mood; this infuriated me.

We fought over control of money. Smaller, more inconsequential control issues could just as easily set us off. One Sunday after breakfast, Carlos suggested we pack a picnic, pile in the car, and go for a drive.

"So where are we headed?" I asked, the kids and the picnic basket in the backseat, the four of us ready to roll.

"Why is that something you need to know?" answered Carlos as he gripped the steering wheel and stared straight ahead without starting the car.

"I don't 'need' to know," I said. "But why won't you tell me? Hey wait, do you have a surprise for us?"

Carlos turned to face me. "No," he said. "There is no surprise." He then turned his face away to start the car, and we began a silent drive to a destination I don't remember.

Me hizo comer hielo.

Again he took to going out alone at night, again with no explanations offered. As in Costa Rica, he never admitted to other women, and I never learned of any. I had already adopted a policy that I still swear by: "Never ask a question you don't really want the answer to." Adultery wouldn't have been the cause of death in our marriage, anyway. For me, it was hypothermia, from all the icy stares, minus the warmth of words of explanation and respect for my feelings. Carlos and I limped along for five more years and then divorced.

Fast-forward through six years of single parenting in Colorado and New Mexico to meeting Joe and experiencing my second long-term relationship. And my second ethnic experience as well. Missionaries in Cameroon, West Africa, had given him the name of Joseph; his parents had named him Bongabe. Joe was a multilingual engineer with a doctorate degree, educated in

Paris and Berkeley. And he was the eldest son, destined to return home to a position as tribal chief.

I don't think I learned much about myself from my experience with Carlos. Here I was again, crediting myself with being some kind of internationalist, as I entered my second serious cross-cultural relationship, this one even more exotic than the first. I loved to fantasize about living in Africa as a quasi-royal. The reality of being the partner of a displaced, would-be chief was something else entirely. It meant serving as hostess at a never-ending Open House. African friends, students, and new arrivals came and went freely from his house in New Mexico, along with some American hangers-on. The kitchen never closed, and filled early and often with people cooking or waiting to be fed. A meal, a place to sleep, a loan, a ride, a good time—these things were expected from Joe and therefore from me as his partner.

At first the lifestyle seemed fascinating and fun. I was right in there, up until all hours, throwing back my fair share of cheap champagne, these Africans' drink of choice. And roasting a goat in your backyard—how cool was that? But with no previous experience at communal living, I soured on it fast. For me, the lack of privacy, the long hours of socializing, and the what's-mine-is-yours attitude that Joe expected me to have were impossibilities. I didn't have in me the requisite tolerance or energy.

Joe apparently found this being surrounded by people and providing for them exhilarating. If the needy didn't call him, he called them and invited them over. In the end, it was an irreconcilable difference between us. He said he would try to create some boundaries if I followed him to Massachusetts and we shared a house. I wanted to believe him, but in truth I half expected what turned out to be a greater invasion of people on the East Coast, with its higher density of immigrants and students.

I was disappointed, however. Over the course of a few months, I went from sad to cold to hostile, and finally holed up in my bedroom like a guerrilla fighter, ready to pounce on these foreign invaders and drive them out of my homeland by force. Joe turned disdainful and called me a spoiled woman incapable of sharing, small-spirited, close-minded. Soon he and I couldn't talk to each other without heating up to a scream fest, often in front of an audience that many times included my children.

I had to leave, to get my own place. To do that, I had to find a job. After four months of unsuccessful looking, I was becoming frantic. Snowstorm or not, they would have had to barricade the Springfield-to-Worcester highway and line it with explosive devices to keep me from that interview at Jamesbury with Marsh Greene. Listening to him now, over lunch at the Publick House, I tried to hide my anxiety and focus on winning him over.

After the lunch dishes were cleared, Marsh brought up the subject of compensation. If you have to break some bad news, you can do worse than in a colonial inn, before a warming fire, after a meal of scrod and Indian pudding. He said he felt embarrassed to tell me what the company was offering. It came to exactly half my last salary in Denver, plus a ho-hum benefits package and nothing else—no stock options, no perks. He said he'd been unsuccessful in negotiating for more. I believed him. The need, the setting, the appeal of the man who was to be my boss all overpowered me. *Oh, what the hell,* I thought. "If I am fortunate enough to be offered this job, I will take it," I said.

A few interviews later and a week before Christmas, I started work. Day one was the day our unit, Human Resources, had its gift exchange. Nobody knew me, of course, and it didn't bother me to lie low in my office while the others opened their presents. But apparently it bothered Marsh, because he slipped out and bought something for me: an oversized green coffee mug filled with red plastic poinsettias. I couldn't help it; my eyes filled with tears at the kindness of his gesture. He covered for me and said, "Yeah, it is a pretty tacky gift and enough to make you cry. I'm a bad shopper, even if I had remembered the gift exchange today."

Jamesbury proved to be as unchallenging as I needed it to be. Despondent over the end of my relationship with Joe, unsure of myself as a parent after forcing my kids to leave schools and friends they liked, and tired from a three-hour commute every day, I needed to excel in at least one arena without its taking too much out of me. Jamesbury was small and unsophisticated. It was friendly, too, and old-fashioned. The company bowling league started up in January, the golf league in May. The family picnic happened in August. The week before Thanksgiving, all of us stood in line and filed by Howard, that short, balding, Jewish guy I had envisioned Marsh to be. He had started the company (in his garage, of course) and had since retired. But he came back every year to shake the men's hands and kiss the women on the cheek, making small talk with many of the longtime employees. The company president stood nearby and handed each of us a twelve-pound frozen turkey as we passed by; we made some more small talk, then went back to our desks and machines.

Marsh was turning out to be a great boss. We worked together as partners, mainly because he'd never had a senior-level woman reporting to him and he didn't know how to deal with me. So he just did what came naturally, which was to treat me as his equal.

The nervous energy passing between us filled whatever space Marsh and I shared. We were in and out of each other's offices constantly, sharing our latest and greatest insight about the company, the job, or life in general. I convinced myself it was the exciting work that made me too agitated to sit close to him when in his office, and him unable to sit down at all when in mine. That it was not unusual to be staring at my boss when he wasn't looking, admiring his fine-boned wrists and the turn of his rolled-up shirtsleeve.

For a year, we were joined at the hip. We co-developed programs. We co-chaired committees. We co-presented at meetings. We were each other's sounding board, editor, audience, and biggest supporter. Most Fridays we crossed the street to T. O. Flynn's for a few beers, always as part of a group, but also always making sure the other was going to be there. "So what do you think? Joining us for a pop at T.O.'s?" he'd ask at 4:45. "I'm thinking about it," I'd answer as I released the knot in my stomach that had been forming since 4:30.

I told myself we were just colleagues who liked each other a lot. Of course I felt attracted to a self-effacing, quick-witted, high-energy man who enjoyed my company; who wouldn't be? He hadn't said or done anything inappropriate. I would have been disappointed in him if he had. It embarrassed both of us to hear later that co-workers had assumed we were lovers. For me personally, sleeping with the boss was tacky and out of the question. As a woman and single parent, it also would have been dangerous. It's the junior woman, not the senior man, who risks getting the hook.

Plus the timing was off. As Marsh told me after I left the company, he, too, was wrung out. In 1978, his wife of more than thirty years had left him, come back three months later, stopped taking medication for depression, and attempted suicide. Counseling hadn't helped, and the best they had managed for the past seven years was a tense, silent impasse. They agreed to divorce, and proceedings had begun. For my part, I was coming home after a long drive to unhappy teenagers who were justified in hating their substandard schools and who hadn't made new friends yet.

I needed to move Jennifer and Michael into better schools and to live closer to work. I'd been in Massachusetts for a year but knew next to nothing about Worcester or the surrounding small towns. Marsh offered to show me around one Saturday and to give me his opinions. I met him in the Jamesbury parking lot, and we took off in his battered blue pickup.

Marsh had chosen a handful of small towns to show me—Northborough, Southborough, Westborough, Marlborough, Grafton, Boylston, Princeton, Westminster, Hopedale, and Hopkinton. He gave measured descriptions of them while I stared out the window. Westborough had the highest-ranking school district in the area a few years back, he said, and still ranked in the top three. Hopedale had new affordable housing going in, meaning more newcomers like me and my kids.

Southborough was a bedroom community of commuters to Boston, full of professional people who kept to themselves. Grafton had more churches than restaurants, and its "hysterical society" enforced stringent restrictions on home owners. Princeton, where he lived, was home to a ski resort and many tennis courts built by him and his son, Jeff, as a side business.

I was grateful for Marsh's help and tried to tell him. But the words stuck in my throat, and I had to fight to keep from crying. I felt scared and alone. For me, this was another move, another failed relationship, another change of school for Jennifer and Michael, more faking in front of them that I knew what I was doing and that we'd be okay. I had no one here to confide in, either. No family members lived in New England. The closest thing to a friend was my boss, and I wasn't about to unload even more of my personal life on him. But Marsh understood. He looked at my face, then took his hand, rested it on top of mine on the seat between us, and left it there while he continued with his running commentary.

Two Saturdays later, he was waiting to help me unpack in Westborough, which I chose because of its top-rated high school and a townhouse I could afford to rent. After he left, I took the kids for lobster to celebrate. It was a dumb idea. Too late for lunch and too early for dinner, we sat in the darkened restaurant by ourselves, barely talking to each other. What could any of us say that would ease the anxiety we felt? The three of us had no talent for false cheer. The "new start" in Springfield qualified as our personal worst in their childhoods filled with new starts. Things could only look up, but still, my confidence was shot, and Jennifer and Michael felt it, barometers that kids turn into when it comes to their parents' moods.

I have smart children. "We instinctively knew better than to question your judgment," Jennifer said years later, when we reminisced about that traumatic time in our lives. "It wasn't in our best interest to undermine our only source of support."

When the lobsters came out, I was too numb to eat mine. The kids didn't know how to use the crackers to open theirs, and I didn't know how to show them.

Several months later, someone told me that Marsh had left his home and was living nearby with his old friend Gus. We didn't talk to each other about our personal lives. In addition to my fear of being unprofessional with my boss, I think we sensed that each of us had wounds to lick and resting up to do. But the unacknowledged sexual tension between us was becoming unbearable. We each tried to control it. We stopped running back and forth between offices. He divided the meetings and presentations between us "so we can cover more ground." I came up with excuses for not being available for beers at T.O.'s.

The strain of working in offices across from each other all but crippled me. I ached for Marsh's attention. But he didn't seem to miss mine. I glowered at him through my window as he scribbled on a yellow legal pad day after day, head down, not noticing my glare. Couldn't he at least look up once in a while and offer me a weak smile? Would that have compromised him so much? He didn't care about me; that was it. I had mistaken what passed between us as chemistry. I was a pathetic idiot.

"Oh, I felt you staring at me, all right," he told me, when giving his side of the story. "But I couldn't trust myself to look up and not do something ridiculous, like blow you a kiss."

Marsh broke the ice. We learned that both of us would be required to attend a seminar in Florida in April. He was reading a memo about it when I came into his office. He swiveled his chair to face me, held my gaze, and said, "If we go to Florida, you know we'll sleep together." I said, "Yes, I know," and then walked out. Amazingly, it seems to me now, we left it at that. We didn't speak about it or spend time alone with each other for days. But there it was—admitted, mutual, to be dealt with.

I knew I had to leave Jamesbury. This time I took the initiative and called a headhunter. I got lucky and landed a new job in three weeks. It was a good one, too, with a Fortune 100 biotech company outside of Boston: more responsibility, more challenging work, more money. I handed my resignation to Marsh on a Wednesday. That Friday we sat on a log with a six-pack of beer, next to Lake Chauncey in Westborough, holding hands and kissing. A fifty-three-year-old father of three and a thirty-eight-year-old mother of two, acting like a couple of timid teenagers. It would become one of my first entries in "Remember the Sweet Things."

# Chapter 2

## *Courtship:*
## *1985—1987*

MARSH AND I DIDN'T DATE, HE COURTED ME. HE
was an old-fashioned romantic who wrote letters to
thank me for lovely evenings together. He sent roses to
my office to celebrate our one-month "anniversary" and
tulips on the first day of spring. He held my elbow when
we crossed streets, pulled out my chair in restaurants,
and stood up when I came back into a room.

It might sound stuffy, but it didn't feel that way. Both
of us were starved for kindness and understanding, and
grateful for one more chance at romance. Over and over
he would tell me I was thoughtful, perceptive, witty,
and pretty. That my strength of character inspired him.
That he loved listening to my intelligence. I told him
he was charming, kindhearted, exciting, and insightful.
That his many talents amazed me. That the skillful-
ness of his lovemaking had me daydreaming. It wasn't

shameless flattery; we each meant every word. And it felt so good and was so much fun to say the words out loud.

One of our first real dates was a road trip to Providence. Months earlier I had mentioned seeing the musical *Evita* on four different stages and said I would see it again any chance I got. He remembered and reserved tickets for a Saturday night performance when the show came to Providence.

"Let's make a day of it," he suggested, "and I'll show you some more of my home turf."

Early that sunny autumn Saturday afternoon, we roared down country back roads, headed for Rhode Island. This time, instead of his beat-up blue truck, he drove his beat-up lime green Porsche, its seats covered in sheepskin. It was an old Porsche 920 that spent a lot of time in the shop; we heard all about it at work every time he came in late. The racket made by that car was well known to cops throughout Worcester County.

"I've been pulled over so often for speeding, a couple of them smile and call me by name when they write me up," Marsh said.

First we drove by the house he grew up in and that his mother had moved out of a few years before. It was a stately one-hundred-year-old white colonial with dark green shutters, surrounded by a sea of manicured grass. The house looked out over Providence Bay and the

Rhode Island Country Club, where the family had a membership for the past forty years. His room had been a third-floor garret.

"I slept in that room all through grade school and high school," he said. "Until I finally moved away from home at age twenty. And then only into a fraternity house."

"You sound embarrassed about that," I said.

"Yeah, well, I think I was kind of a mamma's boy. Maybe she even thought so. I know she'd had it with me when I was eleven and still believed in Santa Claus. She refused to take me to see him at Shepherd's Department Store that year and was exasperated with me for having to explain why." Both of us smiled.

We drove on and into the city, passing the mammoth wrought-iron front gate of Brown University. "Here's my alma mater," he announced. His father, grandfather, and great-grandfather had also graduated from Brown, and his mother from its then sister school, Pembroke.

He was a legacy, true, he said, but hastened to add he had attended on a Navy ROTC scholarship. He thought he owed it to his parents because of a car accident. It was 1949. Within days of getting his driver's license, he skidded on wet leaves and totaled their 1937 Buick. He was mortified, he said, and felt terrible guilt. Years later he figured out the car probably was worth all of a hundred dollars.

"But I loved 'the Senior Service,'" he said. "Wouldn't have minded being a lifer, actually. But I kept it to four years of active duty, then twenty more in the reserves. You can call me 'Commander' if you want, but only here in the car." That earned him a peck on the cheek.

Next up was Old Harbor Marina, where we stopped and got out of the car.

"I have a surprise," he said as he pulled a basket out of the trunk. "I thought you might enjoy a picnic supper before the play."

He carried the basket and held my hand as he led me down a dock lined with sailboats, their masts dipping in the late-afternoon breeze. He stopped in front of a high-sided boat with sturdy, clean lines that looked seaworthy even to me, who'd never been on a sailboat before. "Welcome aboard *St. Kilda*," he said as he helped me step onto the afterdeck. He and a partner had just bought her, and he was proud of her and her story. She was a forty-foot pilothouse sloop, he said, designed by a well-known English boat architect named Lauren Giles, built for the harshness of the North Sea, and named for her maiden voyage to St. Kilda, the outermost island of the Hebrides, off the coast of Scotland.

"A sixty-year-old British farmer commissioned her," Marsh said. "He'd never sailed before, and there he was, with another old farmer friend, heading for a deserted island, across three hundred nautical miles of rough sea," he said, respect in his voice. We headed down to the galley, where he pointed out a faded photo on the wall of *St. Kilda* the boat anchored off St. Kilda the island.

I fell in love with the galley on the spot. The banks of finely finished mahogany cabinets with latches shiny as coins fresh from the mint, the gimballed two-burner stove swaying to the rhythm of waves lapping against the hull, the tiny icebox just big enough for a couple of six-packs and probably deemed sufficient by British warm-beer drinkers. The galley intrigued me—such a handsome, economical use of space. I liked the layout of the two en-suite sleeping cabins, too, one on either end of the boat, maximizing privacy.

"Wow," I said. "The bathrooms even have showers. Is that unusual on a ship this size?"

"Okay, let's start making a sailor out of you," Marsh said. The bathroom was called a head, and a vessel the size of *St. Kilda* was a boat, he explained. And, by the way, a boat measuring forty feet or more qualifies as a yacht. "Its sounding pretentious to call your boat a yacht, well, that's something else again," he said.

We moved to the afterdeck, where I sat staring at the sun as it began to set and Marsh went down to the galley to ready the supper he had started at home. He'd given me a lot to think about. In the year and a half I'd known him, he never so much as hinted at a pedigree, other than dropping the fact of the family's arrival from England in the 1600s. Of course I knew he was a classy guy. Now he seemed almost intimidating. What was I doing standing on the deck of a boat with an Ivy League, Son of the American Revolution, Navy commander? The only thing wrong with this picture was my being in it. I was in culture shock. Intra-American culture this time, but alien, nevertheless, to the daughter of midwestern blue-collar parents who met on a factory floor.

Marsh popped up from the galley with a cheery "Here I am again." In one hand he carried a tray filled with stuffed mussels, in the other an opened bottle of red wine and two plastic wineglasses.

"Stuffed mussels are my signature starter," he said. "You might be eating a lot of them."

*From your lips to God's ears,* I thought.

Marsh placed a mussel shell in my hand and the shock began to wear off. Hell, why not me, sitting on the afterdeck of a gorgeous boat with a handsome man, sipping a Spanish rioja and savoring seafood fixed especially for me, as we watched the sunset. If only he had arranged for a camera crew so there would be pictures to prove this had happened to me.

"Tell me more about your roots," I said, settling back into my deck chair, relaxing as the rioja took effect. I was hoping my first Olde Yankee would slip a little American history into his stories about the family.

He didn't disappoint. Marshall Whitney Greene

could trace his lineage back to the first Pilgrim settlers of the Massachusetts Bay Colony. A cousin still lived in a family home built in 1691 in Westminster, amid the hills and pine forests of Central Massachusetts. He and his historian wife had restored the horsehair plaster walls and replanted the original English garden, following the design they found among some yellowing old papers. Captured Hessian soldiers were imprisoned in the barn during the Revolutionary War; they worked the fields during and after the war.

There were some illustrious relations. A distant cousin, Eli Whitney, was born in Westborough and went on to invent the cotton gin. An uncle, Harry Emerson Fosdick, was one of America's premier radio preachers in the 1930s and founder of John D. Rockefeller's Riverside Church in Manhattan. An aunt, Amy Greene, started the social work program at the American University of Beirut in Lebanon. And Marsh came by his sentimentality rightly, it turned out. His great-grandfather, George C. Whitney, started the Whitney Valentine Company in 1865, at the tail end of the U.S. Civil War. He grew it into one of the country's largest producers of Valentine's Day cards before it folded in the 1940s, due to a paper shortage caused by World War II.

"Your turn now," Marsh said.

I had no people of note to offer. My stock was the

typical midwestern mix of Irish and German immigrant farmers who managed modest upward mobility. The second generation received a bit of schooling, left the farm, and moved to town. The third generation made it through high school and sold off the farm. The fourth generation, mine, became the family's first college graduates, and many of us left town and the state altogether.

Nor did we have any particularly colorful reprobates. The closest we came was a bootlegger grandpa, my mother's father, Tom Finnerty. During Prohibition in the 1920s, he and his brother Matt brought Canadian whiskey over the border into northern Wisconsin and stored it in a shed next to Matt's house, which sat on top of a hill. My mother and her brothers were grade school kids then and loved it when their father announced it was time once again to drive up and spend a few days with their cousins. They especially liked the midnight game their father and uncle arranged for them all to play, rousting them out of bed and urging them on in whispers, as the kids rolled barrels down the hill to waiting trucks bound for Chicago.

Their reward was a predawn Irish fry-up of eggs, bacon rashers, sausages, potatoes, and tomatoes, cooked by their sullen, silent mothers before sending them back to bed.

Marsh liked that story. He would ask me to tell it often during the course of our years together.

That daylong date in Providence kicked off the magical summer of 1985. I could hardly write fast enough to capture all the Sweet Things for the list I had started. A candle-lit dinner in the kitchen of friend Gus's red farmhouse. A weekend at an old inn in the White Mountains of New Hampshire. A stroll down Beacon Street after dinner at the Parker House. Flowers, movies, phone calls "just to say good night"—all for me, from a personable, considerate man with a kiss as sweet as Boston cream pie.

It was movie script romantic, and Marsh made a great leading man. I couldn't stop gazing at him or telling him how attractive he was. I knew it was shallow of me to keep harping on his looks, but I couldn't seem to help myself, even though it embarrassed him. Like his boat, *St. Kilda,* he had classic good lines: a shapely head with a nicely rounded back, a high forehead, a strong jaw, deep-set eyes, ears close to his head. In repose, his face seemed on the verge of a smile. Probably because he smiled readily, with a great smile that lit up his eyes and warmed you on contact. "I am likable. You can trust me," his smile said.

He had a full head of salt-and-pepper hair that turned soft and fluffy after shampooing. He liked that I couldn't resist giving it a gentle pat when I passed his chair. "If you lose your hair, we're through," I told him.

He looked comfortable in his clothes and moved

like the natural skier and tennis player he was—fluidly, with quick reflexes. He landed gracefully if tripped up, but usually managed to keep himself upright. "Like a mountain cat," he would kid after near misses. I felt protected when walking with him, in safe hands, as if he could stop me from falling, too, just by being there next to me.

There were imperfections. A bit too broad in the beam and made to look broader by thin shoulders. Piano legs with skinny ankles and knees crisscrossed with surgical scars. Mountain cat or not, he had experienced enough spills on boat decks and tennis courts for them to take their toll. Stubby fingers untouched by a manicurist; gnarled toes best kept hidden from view. Yet anyone taking him in, top to bottom, would have agreed with me that he was one good-looking man. I felt proud to be on his arm.

Jennifer and Michael were proud to be associated with Marsh, too. He invited the three of us for a sail to Block Island one September weekend and told the kids they could each invite a few friends to come along. He let them all take turns at the helm and taught them a few things, like how to trim a sail and cleat a line. My kids hung around him, asking questions and encouraging him to tell some stories they'd already heard; they were showing him off.

We had glorious weather that trip—sunny with light

winds. The girls put on swimsuits and lay sunning on towels spread out on the foredeck. The boys set up fishing lines back aft and talked big about catching dinner. No worries there—I had provisioned for a trans-Atlantic passage. We hauled aboard cases of soft drinks, a giant duffle stuffed with cookies and chips, an Igloo cooler mounded with cold cuts and cheeses. I brought along so much orange juice, you'd think I expected an outbreak of scurvy on our two-day sail.

When we reached Block Island and anchored, the kids rowed in to check out the funky little beach town. Marsh and I stayed behind to watch the other boats come in, enjoy a sundowner, and cook a pasta dinner for eight. At home later the next evening, the three of us by ourselves, suntanned and happy, my kids and I declared the weekend to be one of our best ever. Marsh called to say he felt the same.

I floated through the next couple of days on a wave of contentment after that fabulous weekend and didn't think anything of not hearing from him until Wednesday, when he called me at work. He asked if he could come over after dinner to speak with me. To speak with me? Of course he could "speak" with me. What did we need to "speak" about? He was scaring me.

When I opened the front door and saw his face, I knew I had good reason to be scared. He looked anxious, his eyes darting back and forth between my face and his feet. He held his arms folded across his chest and kept his distance, instead of his usual way of taking my hands in his and leaning in to give me a gentle kiss hello.

"Where are the kids?" he asked, his voice solemn.

"Upstairs in their rooms," I said. I thought, *Why does he want to know that? Does this involve them? What have we done? Oh God, what's happened?* We went into the living room and sat on the sofa; Marsh turned to face me and began.

Janet had changed her mind about the divorce. She told him she couldn't make it without him. She didn't love him or respect him, she said; this much she had told him before. But she needed him now, she realized, and was afraid for herself if he weren't there for her, as he had been for thirty-two years. She knew about me.

He stopped talking and reached for my hands while tears filled his eyes. I gathered him in my arms and held him. He cried silently, his face pressed against my chest, his body shaking; after a few minutes, he was calm.

"I don't know what to do," he said. "I'm so sorry, El. But I owe her. It's my duty. I just don't know what to do. I know what I want, and that's to be with you. But I think I have to go home. It's my duty," he repeated.

I can't remember what I said. Not much of anything, I think, I was too numb with disbelief. I remember we cried together, sitting there on my sofa holding hands.

Then he got up and let himself out. Jennifer and Michael came downstairs. They must have overheard at least something of what we had said, because Jennifer asked what happened. I didn't share much, saying merely that Marsh might not be coming back. That was unkind of me, regardless of my motivation to spare them the sad news. They had invested in Marsh, too. It was the three of us whom he had captivated, this dream man who had opened a door to a world of fun and affection we had gone years without. Now he had slammed the door and walked away, and I wasn't telling them why.

He sent flowers the next day. And called in the evening to say he left work at noon that day, too sick to his stomach to stay. I had done the same and spent the afternoon in bed crying. We called each other often over the next few weeks and spent torturous hours on the phone. He was talking to Janet almost every day, too, but still staying at Gus's house. His anguish was palpable as he talked in circles about his confusion. Always it focused on duty and selfishness—what he should do versus what he had a right to do.

"I took a vow," Marsh said. "I promised to be there, for better or for worse. Janet is sick. I know she needs me. How can I break my word now, when she's begging me to stay? What kind of man does that make me?"

"An arrogant one," I answered. "You think it's all

up to you to make Janet happy. You don't possess that power. She's made that clear to you." Harsh, unsympathetic words from someone conniving to make her own case.

Marsh didn't respond; it probably sounded like so much psychobabble to him. I didn't believe in what I said, either; in truth, I found his angst admirable. Just as I admired his not sharing much about Janet or their marriage, even when I pried. He was loyal to his wife, and I respected him for that. But he had told me that he felt responsible in part for her chronic depression, undiagnosed for decades.

"She had three babies in five years and too much time alone with them, while I was out playing 'young-man-on-the-rise,'" Marsh said. "My job, the Junior Chamber of Commerce, the United Way, Worcester County politics, Unitarian Church Sunday school—you name it, I gave it my time. On top of that, a month in the summer and eleven weekends a year to the Navy. Not much time left for my wife and kids." After what he had put her through, maybe he deserved her hard feelings toward him, he reasoned.

But he also asked himself if he deserved to endure another thirty years of paying the price for past mistakes. He had vowed to have and to hold, but what about the other vow that Janet admitted she couldn't keep, in which they promised to love and to cherish each other? Should Marsh hold himself to one promise while allowing Janet to excuse herself from another? And what good had it done her to stay in a loveless marriage of convenience? His presence in the past hadn't resulted in her happiness; what difference was it apt to make in the future? For me, of course, the answers were clear. But not for Marsh, who struggled with these questions and came to different conclusions, based on the strengths of Janet's and my arguments during our many hours of agonized phone conversation with him.

Finally he sought professional help, and Rudy, a counselor he and Janet had seen before, came up with a plan. Marsh was to cut off contact with Janet and me in order to sort out his own feelings and needs. The anguish the three of us suffered was made worse by us women pleading our cases with him, which in turn exacerbated his guilt and indecisiveness. He was to set a deadline and not allow himself to wallow in indecision indefinitely. The deadline was New Year's Day.

I barely functioned during three months of self-imposed solitary confinement. I went to work, came home, made dinner, and stared at the TV until I fell asleep in front of it. Jennifer and Michael left me alone, and I rarely reached out to them. I was too afraid of the hurt their questions might cause me.

This behavior was not like me. I didn't shut down when my love life was less than perfect. I didn't isolate myself just because a man had entered or exited my life. I had too much else to do. I built a career and raised happy kids for the better part of ten years by myself. The three of us had full lives: Scouts, day camps, and get-togethers with friends for the kids; the National Organization for Women, Women's Political Caucus, and hiking or cross-country skiing with mountain clubs for me. Most weekends, the three of us went to the library, to the movies, and out to dinner, where we loved the search for new places to try. It was a routine we looked forward to.

I even had another man interested in me whose company I could have enjoyed. An engineer at Jamesbury, divorced, raising by himself a daughter a few years younger than Michael, he and I had a lot in common. But he couldn't compete with someone as special as Marsh. Marsh had everything I wanted in a partner. He was funny and fun to be with, self-confident and sexy, hardworking and dependable. He respected me and he liked my kids.

Nevertheless, in mid-November, the halfway point, I gave up on waiting for him to make up his mind. In a terse letter, I told Marsh to take me out of the running. I told him I felt demeaned, nervously waiting to be the lucky lady, picked by a man I was giving the power to break my heart. I had to move on, I wrote, and I wished him well in doing the same. Janet was using similar words, he told me later, and at about the same time.

But I didn't mean what I wrote. I wanted to win. He was the best man I had ever loved, and I wanted him. I was indeed waiting for him, whether I admitted it to him or myself. In mid-December, he sent us a Christmas box of books he had selected and inscribed. I felt ecstatic with relief. Maybe he hadn't taken me at my word. Plus his gift granted me permission and enough time to send him a Christmas present, too. To love celebrating Christmas as much as I do and not be able to share even one small part of it with Marsh had bothered me for weeks. I baked batches of his favorite lemon squares and oatmeal cookies and mailed them off.

The kids and I took the train to Virginia to spend the holidays with my family. We arrived home by early evening on January 1. I forced myself to keep busy. I fixed us some sandwiches, unpacked all our bags, and started a load of laundry before retreating to my room, wound too tight to concentrate on my book, willing the phone to ring. By 10 P.M., when Jennifer and Michael came up to bed, Marsh hadn't called. He never called me after ten; he considered it rude to call that late. It was over. He was gone. I was devastated.

I had trusted him so completely. He had been so endearing. I had felt so special. How could I have been so wrong? How could he be so cruel? How could he not choose me?

At 11 P.M., a soft knock at the front door startled me. Don't think it, don't hope it, don't set yourself up for the disappointment, I tried to caution myself as I flew down the stairs and opened the door to Marsh, standing under the porch light. He looked gaunt and drained. He was holding a bottle of champagne.

"Will you have me?" he asked.

If he had been going for a laugh, the moment was too choked with emotion for him to pull it off. I had pictured this homecoming over and over in my head during the last months. I envisioned us falling into each other's arms, smashing our mouths together in hungry kisses, throwing our heads back in uproarious glee. It wasn't like that. Marsh was in pain, and it was written on his face.

I took his hand and guided him into the dark kitchen. Turning on a light, I looked into his eyes while holding his ashen face in my hands. We gave each other a long, deep kiss and embraced, rocking back and forth in each other's arms in silence.

We opened the champagne. He offered a toast. "To second chances," he said. We sat down in the living room and tried to talk about what we endured the past three months. But it didn't seem to matter now. Or later; we rarely spoke of that excruciating time in our relationship. It felt pointless to revisit all the sadness and angst. After half an hour, both of us had exhausted what we needed to say. Marsh said he had to go. Back to his room at Gus's, he said, where he hoped he would sleep through the next day, his conscience permitting.

"Maybe I'm giving myself too much credit," he said in a voice dulled by fatigue, "but I don't think I have ever deliberately hurt anyone until tonight." He had come directly from his home in Princeton and explaining himself to Janet.

Why did Marsh choose me? Why was I the one to have my feelings spared? I can't be sure. He didn't offer a detailed explanation.

"I'm a simple guy," he said, "with not too many moving parts. I just want a shot at happiness, and that means being with you."

I can speculate about a deeper level of meaning. I think I represented Marsh's chance for love and respect, the love and respect that Janet said she didn't and couldn't feel for him. In the end, the need for love and respect trumped a sense of duty.

Having a sex life again was part of the definition of love. Marsh was loyal to his wife, as I've said, and didn't betray confidences about their marriage. However, he did let it slip that they had not been intimate "for many, many years." Now along comes a woman who whispers in his ear about the pleasure he gives her and who can't seem to keep her hands off him. Would this not prove irresistible to a man as uncomplicated as Marsh?

As irresistible, I think, as the high esteem in which I held him, personally and professionally. I knew Marsh's Achilles' heel to be his lack of stature at work. Smart enough not to be the nice guy who finished last, he still seemed destined to rise no higher than middle management. This bothered him; he told me so. And it bothered his wife, I learned from others, who said she felt anxious about their social status, based on his lack of a prestigious title.

It didn't bother me a bit. I came from outside his social world, so his place within it carried no weight with me. And I came from inside his work world, where, as a management developer, I understood something about how people got ahead. In my experience, people like Marsh, who possessed few political instincts and no talent for self-promotion, reached a plateau in their careers and stayed there. It didn't reflect on the quality of their work or their intelligence. When Marsh offered the toast "To second chances," I think he meant another chance to see respect in the eyes of a woman who could love him for who he was. She could also be trusted, as any loving spouse should be trusted, to refrain from hitting him in the raw spot where she knew he already hurt.

Whatever the reasons, simple or complex, Marsh had chosen me. And seemed bent on making up for lost time. The next week, over dinner at my house, he announced a plan for celebrating my January birthday. We would meet in Madrid, after my business trip to Mallorca and his to Lisbon conveniently ended within a day of each other. Marsh would arrange everything—hotel, car, places to see. He had lived and worked in Spain in the late sixties, loved the country, and couldn't wait to share with me some parts of it that he considered special.

In easily the most romantic four days of my life, we checked into the elegant old Plaza Hotel and acted like honeymooners, with lots of lolling in bed and morning room service. We rented a car and raced around the Spanish countryside by day, visiting castles and cathedrals and monuments, with Marsh always serving as effusive tour guide. By night, we made the rounds of tapas bars in Madrid, where we sampled tortilla Española and sipped tinto from stout little glasses as we traversed the city. It was sublime.

Back home, we settled into a routine. We spent Tuesday night, Thursday night, and Friday night through Sunday together. Sometimes we just went out for a drink after work. Sometimes one or the other made dinner. Sometimes we sat and read or watched TV. Weekends varied with the season and, for me, were full of newness. Cold months meant drives to Vermont and New Hampshire to stay with friends at their ski houses. I didn't have friends with ski houses. For that matter, I could barely ski. Certainly not well enough to keep up with Marsh. He still taught evening classes at his neighborhood mountain, Mount Wachusett, as he had done for the last twenty years. He showed such classic form going down a hill that the ski school featured him in their promotional video.

Marsh and his friends were accustomed to returning from a day on the slopes to dress for cocktails and dinner. They were old friends and classmates with forty years of joint history who accepted me warmly, but who settled in their chairs before the fire to share reminiscences that couldn't include me. I got used to it.

Warm months meant weekends on the water. This time it was friends' summer houses on Cape Cod and Narragansett Bay, with drinks and dinner after a day of sailing. It was heady stuff for me, and I loved it. I felt conflicted about leaving the kids alone as often as we did, but not enough to deny myself this classy social life.

I felt unsure of myself at the beginning. I listened carefully for clues on what stories to tell about myself. Nothing involving politics or activism; I learned that the hard way. A yellow-dog Democrat and feminist, I was surrounded by conservative Republicans. I outed myself one evening by singing the praises of Ted Kennedy and set myself up for baiting by a few of the men. The baiting turned snide on occasion and made us all uncomfortable. Especially Marsh. He knew how seriously I took my politics. During our first fight, over how he intended to vote in an upcoming local election, I made him swear to change his voter registration from Republican to Independent or we had no future. I don't know if he ever did it. I know I got off my high horse and stopped making outlandish threats. Probably because Marsh wised up and stopped divulging how he voted.

I also felt unsure of myself about something as simple as food. I watched closely to see what kind of meals others cooked, so when it was my turn I could make something appropriate. Appropriate seemed to mean fast and not too fussy. People had dishes they were renowned for. In the winter, Marsh's signature dish was cheese fondue; in the summer, stuffed mussels. His friend Bill's summer specialty was clams Posillipo. Basil shrimp became mine. It was important to me that I not appear to be trying too hard.

Marsh made it all easier. For starters, he didn't seem to care what stories I told or what dishes I cooked. After get-togethers those first years, alone in our room, he often said, "I was proud of you tonight." It sounds rather patronizing now. But I must have needed the praise, because I wrote it down often enough on the Sweet Things list.

I gradually developed more confidence in myself. And I came to know that maybe positive feedback was all I was going to get from him. One night after dinner on *St. Kilda* with two other couples, I tried to pin him down about the new chicken recipe I had tried. Hadn't the chicken gone off slightly? Did he think anyone noticed?

"I think everyone thought it was delicious," he said.

But didn't he think that this new dish hadn't quite measured up?

"I like just about everything you've made so far," he said.

I pressed on. But maybe not this dish as much as some of the others?

"Look, El, you'll have to get your constructive criticism elsewhere," he said and gave me a little kiss on the cheek.

He just wasn't much for criticizing or for taking the inconsequential too seriously, as I was doing. Marsh was an unpretentious guy. He brought a bag lunch to work every day. He went to the library for his reading material. He bought his suits off the rack at Anderson-Little and got $4 haircuts every month for the last fifteen years from Manny, the Italian barber. He had only one of most things in his closet—one gray suit, one navy blue blazer, one leather belt. When his one pair of Timberland boat shoes wore out, he bought another pair. For his birthday that first year we were together, I bought him a sweater. The only sweater I had ever seen him wear was a gray

V-neck, worn thin at the elbows. He opened the box, saw the new teal blue V-neck from L. L. Bean, said thanks, and put it aside.

"Don't you like it?" I asked.

"Sure," he said. "But I already have a sweater."

There was nothing vainglorious about him. I, on the other hand, obsessed about how I looked in Marsh's world. What to wear to the big Friday night cocktail parties in Princeton was my biggest clothing nightmare. For me, they were grim affairs. Forced mingling from 6 to 9 P.M., with too much alcohol on an empty stomach and the group's apparent denial of permission to appear under the influence, given the always decorous behavior of the attendees. Made worse because I knew I was "the younger woman," on the arm of newly divorced Marsh and on display before the hometown crowd. Their kids had grown up together, and they had been in and out of each other's houses for years. They were a sporty set who played mixed-doubles tennis on each other's courts and skied together at Mount Wachusett.

I had little in common with the other women, many of whom were older and didn't work outside the home. Awkward as always at stand-up parties full of strangers, abysmal at small talk, and nervous about the impression I might be making, I didn't dig much to find some common ground. No one treated me unkindly. If anything, I was the one who came predisposed to judge them harshly. I figured them to be spoiled lightweights who'd never had to get a real job. I was wrong: Anne worked full time in Worcester's Antiquarian Society archives; Nancy was the Princeton postmistress; Sue ran her doctor husband's office. But it took me a while to be able to see over the chip on my shoulder.

I wanted to fit in but not enough to take up tennis or change my look. I came straight from the office, dressed in a pencil-straight tight skirt, drapey cashmere sweater, and Colorado cowboy boots. Calculatedly flashy. Most of the other women, relaxed and fresh from the shower at home, showed up in the New England matron's uniform of boiled wool jacket, plaid pleated skirt, and low-heeled pumps. My new clothing goal was to look appropriate but with a twist. Understatement needed to be factored in, too. It seemed de rigueur in this crowd, which made choosing what to wear all the more difficult for me as an outsider who hadn't grown up with the dress code. Some things were obvious, like no costume jewelry. Why else would every female tolerate no more than a single strand of pearls or a simple gold chain around her neck? But how about a pleated skirt with that drapey cashmere sweater—still too flashy? Or a pants suit with those cowboy boots—too world-of-work and in their faces about it? I was almost always late for work on cocktail party Fridays as I tried on outfit after outfit.

Sometimes Marsh witnessed the fashion show. Asking his opinion was a waste of time, of course. It was predictable. He said, "That looks good"; or "You look fine"; or "I like that look." I expected him to become exasperated, which would have made me all the more anxious about caring so much about something so silly. But he never lost patience with me. He was wise enough to sense that this wasn't just about how I looked. It had to do with something more important: my feeling comfortable enough in his world to become his partner for life.

We weren't fooling around here. This was more than monogamy. We had begun to meld our two families.

First Marsh brought me to Rhode Island to meet his mother, Marjorie. She was a lovely woman, demure in her silk blouse and pearls, her silver hair coiffed, her ankles crossed and hands resting in her lap. Marjorie was engaging and open with me.

"My son was unhappily married for many years," she said. "That was hard for Ray and me to witness," referring to Marsh's father, who had died a few years before.

She was trying to put me at ease, and it worked. I started to gush about Marsh: how thoughtful and caring, how generous and helpful, how witty and intelligent he was. Marjorie beamed and leaned forward a bit in her chair.

"He is quite a catch, isn't he?" she said.

Next came my mother, but she didn't make it so easy. Marsh often told the story of their meeting. The kids and I picked her up at the airport in Boston and drove her to Westborough, where Marsh was fixing a welcome-to-New-England meal for her first-time visit: Rhode Island clam chowder, Maine lobster, and Massachusetts butter and sugar corn.

"Mary," he said, opening the front door and holding out his hand to her, "I'm so pleased to meet you."

"I bet you're not," she said.

My mother had come prepared to dislike Marsh. Besides the many other differences of opinion she and I had over the years, here was yet another example of my poor choice of partners. First a Latino who barely spoke English, then an African as black as burned toast, and now a man too old for me.

"If you marry him, you'll be his nursemaid and his widow," she said.

"If that happens, he'll have been worth it," I countered.

But Mother couldn't dislike Marsh; nobody disliked Marsh. He disregarded the disapproval in the air and continued with his plan of an outing on *St. Kilda* and dinner at his house in Princeton, both of which she enjoyed. I had warned him that Mother's specialty was spotting "phonies," her word for anyone who, in her view, showed excessive polish and charm. So he took care not to fill vacuums in conversation or tell more about himself than she asked. By the end of her stay, he had won her begrudging approval.

The rest of our respective families showed more enthusiasm and support. Marsh's three children, all adults and away from home, met me and my teenagers. My two brothers met Marsh. I met Marsh's two sisters. The get-togethers were friction free and harmonious. I had the feeling that most everyone was simply relieved that both of us had finally fallen in love with someone who saw the same good qualities they had always seen.

Within six months as a couple, Marsh was beginning sentences with "When we get married . . ." This didn't surprise me; I took it for granted, too, that a wedding was in our future. I wasn't nervous when he became more affectionate with Jennifer and Michael, offering to drive them back and forth to their friends' houses and hugging them goodbye when he left to go home. They called him "Marshmallow" and appeared pleased to see him at the breakfast table after he had spent the night. I harbored no doubts about him or fear that he might take off on them again and break their hearts.

I could trust him. Plans didn't get canceled; it was safe to anticipate. If on Tuesday he asked me out for dinner and a movie on Saturday, it happened, always. He would have made the restaurant reservation, gone to the ATM, gassed up his car, and picked me up when promised. Or earlier. The week after Thanksgiving, we could talk about Christmas, and I could tell my brother in Virginia that Marsh would be joining us for the holidays. Weeks before Easter, he could tell his mother to plan on three more for dinner. There was no uncertainty, no need to feel apprehensive that such talk about the future was presumptuous. Some people might have taken all that dependability for granted, but not me. I had never had it so good.

This was intoxicating for me, after years of single parenting and absentee men for partners. It was new for both of us, this being able to count on our partner so completely. Not just to pick up some potatoes at the store as asked or mail the letter as promised. I could count on Marsh to be reasonable. When I said, for instance, that it made me feel guilty to spend the upcoming weekend with him and away from my kids for the second time that month, he understood. "Yeah," he said, "parenting has to be Job One," and then suggested a day trip instead. No trying to talk me out of my feelings, no sulking.

Marsh could count on me to speak up. He appreciated this, after years of living with a depressed wife silently stockpiling grievances. So, when he started to bring work home and pull it out after dinner, I said, "It hurts my feelings to be ignored for paperwork. You have to stop." He agreed in general practice but hoped that exceptions could be made, that I could accept and not personalize some inevitable professional urgencies. I agreed. No call for unspoken resentment on my part; no need for hours of discussion. They were wonderful, these calm conversations and satisfying conclusions.

They set a pattern for the way we functioned over the years, too. We resolved differences quickly, within minutes typically. The handful of times that didn't happen, both of us became sick to our stomachs and couldn't eat until we made up. We didn't spend much time "working" on our relationship, either, in the sense of talking about how we were doing or developing as a couple. There didn't appear to be a need. Neither of us was introspective by nature; maybe we didn't analyze the marriage much because we simply weren't any good at it. Maybe we didn't see things that called for improvement. Or maybe there weren't many worthy of note. I know I always felt very proud of Marsh, his behavior, and in particular his behavior toward me, especially when out in public. He said he felt the same about me.

But no matter the harmoniousness of our courtship, after a year and a half of traveling between houses an hour apart, I had had enough. Plus, Jennifer would be a senior at Westborough High School, with only one more year at home before leaving for college. I dearly wished to spend it as a family under one roof and told Marsh so.

I think Marsh would have been content with our Tuesday-Thursday-weekend arrangement for a while longer. He almost came out and said as much. From his perspective, after thirty-two years in a first marriage, we were moving at breakneck speed. What if I changed my mind as I got to know him, he asked. As Janet had done. As I had done with Carlos and Joe. But I felt confidence enough for us both. I used the Sweet Things list to try to make my case.

"I have twelve sheets of entries to prove you're the man for me," I said.

It was flip but true, and Marsh wanted to believe me. We agreed it was time for us to take the next big step.

## "Remember the Sweet Things"

· after a pleasant evening and a dinner I'd fussed over, sending flowers to my office with a note, "Thinking of you and the pasta puttanesca"

· on a warm autumn day in Boston, strolling through Quincy Market, buying scallops and mussels

• on the phone, listening for hours to my rambling accounts of problems at work; offering spot-on advice when asked and not before

• his taking Jennifer on a surprise shopping trip for new ski boots; taking her skiing and giving her a private lesson for her sixteenth birthday

• the first dinner he made for the two of us: stuffed mussels, grapefruit and avocado salad, and Rhode Island clam chowder

• attending the Salisbury Singers' holiday concert at the art museum; a lovely setting and blend of esoteric and familiar Christmas music; he, the handsome bass in the back row in a new tuxedo; his typical self-effacing way with a compliment:

ELLEN: "That was so moving. And I'm sure I heard your voice at least once."
MARSH: "It was probably the time I came in early."

• his sharpening my kitchen knives and fixing the dripping showerhead

• my being a contender for worst student in his twenty-five years of teaching skiing; his encouraging

me ("Think of yourself as a dolphin in a rolling sea . . .")
and not getting exasperated (until I threw my poles)

• our first night sleeping together; at the Hotel Me-
ridien in Boston; his bringing champagne; coffee and
the *Boston Globe* in bed the next morning; the tenderness of his lovemaking

• his way of expressing his opinion, ending with
". . . don't you think?"

• his concern about the delay in getting my mam-
mogram results; sharing with me his feelings of anxiety,
then relief

• calling me the next day to say how much he'd enjoyed himself after a mellow, conversation-filled evening
when we'd felt especially connected

• his returning from a business trip to Mexico City
and bringing Michael some Mexican comic books for
his collection

• a four-day sail around Cutty Hunk and Martha's
Vineyard: leisurely mornings lolling in the forward
cabin; sunny afternoons teaching me to read the wind;
evenings on the afterdeck over cocktails; warming him

up after he bolted out of bed at what he mistook to be the sound of a dragging anchor

• meeting my mother; his making oysters Rockefeller with Michael for dinner, followed by lobster; winning her over when she found him in his kitchen, ironing shirts

• before letting Jennifer take my car, his taking a test drive to check icy road conditions

• his bugging me about renewing my car insurance

• remembering and passing along a compliment from a cantankerous colleague: "Dick told me your new assertiveness course has a wait list, it's so popular."

• the simple comfort of falling asleep and waking up to him, our faces together, smiling ourselves awake

• his easing me into turning forty on January 10 by giving me a present on the tenth of each month for six months prior, the last being the You-Look-Fabulous red dress

• MARSH: "What you often do is turn your *interpretation* of other people's thinking into truths."

ELLEN, smiling: "That's because it *is* truth."
MARSH, smiling: "Omniscience must be a terrible
burden."

• teaching Jennifer how to change a tire

• the countless times he says, "What can I do to
help?" and "I'll do that."

• lugging in a huge damaged crate for training
Simon the Bad News Pound Dog; working with Michael to fix the crate and train Simon

• a summer Sunday bike ride in the country, with a
picnic on Lancaster Common

• our sitting on the sofa watching TV or on the bed
reading; his turning now and again to smile and say, "I
love being with you."

• serving as a kind of straight man, creating open-
ings for me to talk about myself or tell a good story,
in private and with others; bragging about me to his
friends

• his genuine enjoyment of Jennifer's sense of humor;
laughing heartily, encouragingly

• my saying, "I have to go to Michael's baseball game"; his correcting me with "You mean we have to go to Michael's baseball game."

• my meeting his flight from Lisbon, driving him home, then heading for home myself in a snowstorm; his being exhausted and doing jumping jacks outside to stay awake, waiting for the call he insisted I make to tell him I'd gotten home safely

• his sitting at our dining room table, laughing and doing a *TV Guide* crossword puzzle with Michael

• a weekend in Vermont at his old friend's ski house; his making cheese fondue; beaming at me throughout dinner

• humoring me by going with me to do past-life regressing; in his suit and wingtips, under hypnosis, calling up images of himself as an African warrior and a young girl in Germany

• his giving me some sleeping pills to use on a trans-Atlantic flight and writing on the envelope, "May flights of angels sing thee to thy rest."

• when I'd had too much wine and, to quote him, had become "cold-eyed and combative," shutting me up by pinning me down and kissing me hard

• building me some kitchen shelves

• inviting the kids and some of their friends for a weekend on *St. Kilda*; teaching them some of the basics of sailing

• his Bach concert on a Sunday afternoon; taking the four of us for ice cream sundaes afterward

• watching him work the room at a party, listening to people with his eyes, laughing easily and drawing them out by paraphrasing what they'd just said

• the marriage proposal:

ELLEN: "I think this driving back and forth
     between houses has gone on long enough."
MARSH: "Well, what shall we do?"
ELLEN: "I think we should live together."
MARSH: "I can't do that! What would my mother
     think?"
ELLEN: "You're fifty-six. Marjorie is eighty-one."

MARSH: "Well, I guess we have to get married
   then."

   • sailing to Nantucket and celebrating our upcoming December wedding with champagne and dancing in
the pilothouse; his signing off in the passage log, "And
so ends the cruise of the Greenes-to-be."

# Chapter 3

*Newlyweds:*
*1988—1990*

SO WE PLANNED A WEDDING. MARSH WAS RIGHT—— living together wouldn't have suited us. Both of us craved the stability and respectability of a good marriage, and by all indications, ours would be good. I had suggested we live together as the next step in our relationship mainly, I think, because I didn't want Marsh to feel pressured to take the ultimate step of marriage. But twelve years of schooling from the Sisters of Saint Agnes had left their mark. After the debacle with Joe, I knew I couldn't share my bed every night, without benefit of clergy, in plain view of teenaged children, without some nagging sense of shame. It would have felt like unfit behavior for me to be modeling. *For me* to be modeling. I have dear women friends who did a great job of raising lovely children with men they never married, and I respect their decision.

Similarly with Marsh. He said he considered it more honorable, especially at age fifty-six, to live with us as my kids' stepfather than as their mother's boyfriend, or lover, or other label sure to embarrass him. He also liked the idea of being the "official" one and only of a woman who adored him.

"Of course I want to wear a wedding ring," he answered when I asked. "I want everyone to know that I belong to you."

We planned a wedding, and we also bought a house. What a great old house, that first one we lived in together. In Westborough and built in 1780, it was classic barn red with black shutters. We were smitten the minute we stepped onto the original wide pine floorboards in the dining room and heard them creak. Never mind that the house was small—1700 square feet—and needed work.

"All charm and no closets," Marsh said. But neither of us cared.

Marsh checked the Worcester County historical record to find out more about the house. Like many of the old colonials clustered in New England town centers, this one began simply enough with two rooms up and two rooms down—the two bedrooms upstairs separated by the staircase landing; the cooking and eating room downstairs separated from a sitting room by a small square of open space used for birthing babies. Four shallow brick fireplaces provided heat in the low-ceilinged rooms. The wooden shell of an "outhouse" still existed underneath the stairs, down in the dirt-floored cellar.

In 1861, the house was loaded onto horse-drawn logs and rolled down Main Street and around the corner to its current location at 29 West Street. For us, this was a fortuitous turning of a corner. The Historical Society of Westborough concerned itself only with buildings on Main Street, which freed us to make whatever changes we chose. Other people added a few rooms to the back in the late 1880s. But no one, including us, did anything drastic to the original footprint. Probably like the previous owners, we felt responsible for keeping a piece of Americana intact for another two hundred years.

But we had some work to do, and it was more than cosmetic. Down in the cellar, Marsh could make sawdust by poking a screwdriver through the main support beam running down the middle of the house. Eaten away by termites years ago, the beam was as porous as an ocean sponge. It had to be replaced before the house caved in on itself. As it was, pencils rolled off tables and across floors, not stopping until they reached a wall.

Marsh and his son, Jeff, took on the job of raising the midsection of the house by two inches. For twelve hours one Saturday in October, they propped up the house's sagging center on a line of twelve steel posts. The posts sank into the dirt floor and had to be repositioned over and over, until all rested snugly against the rotted-out beam. Then, every night for sixty-four nights, Marsh went down to the cellar and slowly cranked up each post one sixty-fourth of an inch. I held my breath upstairs as the old wooden floors and walls groaned in protest.

Moving on to the cosmetics was more fun. We threw ourselves into them, doing the work ourselves. We were buffing up 29 West for our December wedding, and it was the proverbial labor of love. We stripped off wallpaper in every room and painted or repapered to suit our own taste. We took up boring beige carpeting and refinished all the beautiful pine floors. We tiled bathroom floors and built closet shelves. I cut fabric and made curtains for twenty-two windows. Marsh cut Formica and made new kitchen countertops. Every night and weekend, we worked until one or two in the morning.

The place shone by the big day, December 23, and the Christmas decorating added to its charm. Swags of pine branches hung from every mantelpiece, with sprigs of juniper and holly berries tied on with gold ribbon. Brass candlesticks sat amid more greens decking the mantels, the lit candles made to flicker by the drafty old windowpanes. Shiny red apples, stuck to tall Styrofoam cones with toothpicks and spaces between them filled with holly sprigs, resembled miniature Christmas trees and served as centerpieces on the kitchen and dining room tables. Outside, above our front door and spotlighted from below, was Marsh's re-creation of a colonial holiday favorite: a pineapple, considered a symbol of welcome, centered on a wooden half-circle and surrounded by arches of apples and oranges.

All of our children and grandchildren gathered to share that evening with us: Marsh's daughter Lisa, from Austin; son Jeff and his wife, from upstate New York, with their kids, Tyler, Hannah, and Emily; both of our daughters named Jennifer; and Michael. They joined our mothers, Marjorie and Mary; Marsh's sisters, Marilyn and Julie; my brother Jim; and assorted nieces, nephews, and close friends, as fifty people crowded into our tiny dining room for the ceremony.

We were married in front of a low-burning fire by Jonathan, brother-in-law of our best friends in Westborough. Jonathan was a tall, gaunt-faced Englishman and a minister at Old North Church in Boston. He looked every inch the vicar, whether in or out of his Episcopalian robes. We opted for traditional vows, and Jonathan insisted we each say them in their entirety, as opposed to repeating after him.

"After all," he said, over a glass of port at our house, a few weeks before the wedding, "they are your vows, not mine."

Our recitations were less than stellar. I all but whispered mine, I was so nervous about screwing up and missing a section. And Marsh surprised no one when he broke down while saying his; he'd been known to get teary-eyed during TV commercials. He only made it as far as "I take thee, Ellen, to be my wife . . ." Wedding photographer Gus captured the moment in a great shot of the two of us, pausing for a kiss of encouragement before Marsh gave it another try.

We provided a turkey, a cake, and a bar. The rest was potluck—we asked everyone to bring a favorite dish in lieu of buying a gift. Henrietta, a co-worker of mine who moonlighted as a jazz singer, provided the music. She and her two-man combo set up in the birthing room, while we milled around the rest of the house. It was a congenial, low-key affair that suited us. By 2 A.M., we had said goodbye to the last guests and the house was ours, family having arranged to spend the night with friends. We were in our favorite place, upstairs in our own bed, beginning our married life.

Let me interject that many of the early years entries to "Remember the Sweet Things" recall intimate moments. Not to worry—I won't be burdening you or embarrassing myself by sharing any of them here. What I am sharing are the innocent romantic gestures of two newlyweds in love who acted that way, regardless of their ages. Marsh's blowing me a kiss "goodbye" when the hostess ordered us to separate and sit at opposite ends of the dinner table. My standing next to him in the movie line, running my hand up and down his arm, gazing at him moonily and forcing him to laugh. The two of us, snuggled under the covers one February night, Marsh gently thumping my collarbone with a fingertip and cooing, "My little rose-ate spoonbill. My little white-eared ground sparrow. My little red-breasted guinea hen."

How ridiculous. What nonsense. But what replenishing nonsense it was for two people coming off the desert, spirits half dead from dehydration. And what lovely little memories they provide now, when I encounter them among the entries. The sex was wonderful, especially in those early years, but remembering the silly things is what makes my heart pine.

"It won't be all beer and skittles," Marsh warned several months later, using one of the many old idioms he was fond of. Jennifer kept a running list of them and posted it on a corkboard in the kitchen (like mother, like daughter?). It was springtime, and we were talking over burgers at Harry's Diner about how easily the transition to married life was going.

No doubt he was right—we were bound to have issues. But I was thrilled with my end of the deal so far. Here was a husband who paid the bills, did the laundry, washed the dishes, cleaned the house, and helped me cook. Plus he was handy. He fixed the garbage disposal and sharpened the kitchen knives. He chopped and stacked enough wood for a winter's worth of fires, and built a fine front stoop, complete with handrails. It seemed to me that all I had to do was cook and keep the cookie jar full. I felt guilty, my part looked so easy. But Marsh insisted that I took care of well over 50 percent when it came to the mechanics of our life, which made him the luckier of the two. He meant it. At least he repeated it often enough over the years to convince me of his sincerity. In any event, both of us thinking we were getting the better deal in the relationship made each of us the lucky one.

I loved being Ellen Greene. I loved settling down. The previous twenty years of my life, that is to say all of my adulthood, had revolved around change. I had lived in two countries, four states, six cities, and twelve houses. If I ever kidded that I didn't do windows, it was no joke—we hadn't stayed in one place long enough for it to be necessary. Jennifer and Michael weren't kidding, either, when they called me a change junkie. They had the right. They attended seven different elementary schools and made and lost countless friends, thanks to the moves I subjected them to. Now here I was, in one place for a personal best of five years, and married to a deep-rooted Yankee. Because of Marsh, I belonged to this place in New England. I felt grounded and secure, and I reveled in that feeling.

To be sure, being better off financially played a part. It was great having two nice paychecks instead of one. Not that we turned into Lord and Lady Got-Rocks.

Both of us put in twelve-hour workdays, if you counted the long commutes, for a net gain of a modestly comfortable life. But still, I now had, as Marsh would put it, "a few raisins in the oatmeal." Together we had figured out our expenses and apportioned them according to our salaries, 60 percent Marsh's responsibility, 40 percent mine, with enough left over for each to enjoy some discretionary income. For the first few years, we maintained separate checking accounts, mostly because I didn't want a husband critiquing how I spent "my" money. When it became clear that Marsh wasn't ever going to be that kind of husband, we pooled our salaries in a joint account, and I learned to call the money "ours."

More than the financial security, I felt grounded because I became a member of a set of people, a set who provided the four of us with a social life and a safety net. Marsh had built a network of friends over decades, and enjoyed both personal and professional relationships with them, as happens with people who stay put geographically. Old friend and college buddy Ned managed our portfolio and offered investment advice over the breakfast table in Vermont. Old friend and housemate Gus wrote our insurance policies and handled Michael's fender benders personally. When "my" Jennifer had a minor dustup with the law at UMass, Marsh called Roger, his old friend the lawyer, for some free advice. I called John, his old friend and orthopedic surgeon, who squeezed me in the next day to see about my chronic knee pain.

Marsh took at least some of the special treatment for granted, as evidenced by his taking umbrage at my calling it "special." Friends do for friends, he said. It struck me as more than friends taking care of each other, however. To me, an outsider, these people looked and acted like they owned the place. All they had to do was pick up the phone and call someone for problems to be solved. Your daughter's mortgage loan request was denied? It will go through at a different bank, where a friend sits on the board of directors. Your car insurance lapsed? No problem—send a friend your predated check and he'll take care of everything. You want four tickets to a sold-out affair at the art museum? Your friend the museum docent will set them aside for you.

In other words, Marsh and his friends had influence. Michael and I watched him put it to good use when our car was stolen. Michael had driven Marsh's red Mazda to a party one Friday night in Westborough. Two eighteen-year-olds from Boston broke into it and tried to steal the tape deck, then hot-wired it and drove it to the city, thirty miles away. En route they made the bad decision to stop for a doughnut and a cup of coffee. Also taking a doughnut break were the police officers listening to the APB about our car. They arrested the hapless pair on the spot.

During the next few days, Marsh filled out a police report, his car was dusted for prints and returned, and a court date was set. A week before he and Michael were scheduled to appear in court in Boston, two kids showed up at our backdoor and introduced themselves as Tom and Sean. They sported fresh haircuts and clean, collared shirts.

"We're the clowns who stole your car," said Tom, the taller of the two.

They came to ask if Marsh could see his way to dropping the charges. They would pay for the tape deck they had ruined.

"This is killing my grandpa," said Tom. "Just when I was turning a corner, too. I signed up for the Army. But with a record? I don't think they'll take me."

He wanted to go to Iraq and be a part of Operation Desert Storm, he said. To serve his country; that was all he wanted. His buddy Sean stopped staring at the ground and offered that he wanted to serve his country, too, but his girlfriend was expecting a baby in a few months.

"I should be there for her," he said.

*You're making the wrong pitch as far as I'm concerned*, I thought. *I don't want any U.S. kid to be headed for Iraq, con artist or otherwise.*

Marsh told Tom and Sean he would have to think about it. As they walked away, heading for the highway and a bus back to Boston, he turned to me, smiled, and said, "Oh, what the hell. They're just dumb kids." He was going to drop the charges.

Easier said than done. At the court appearance, which he took off work to attend, he met resistance from the assistant district attorney assigned to the case. Marsh had pressed charges. The kids had been caught dead to rights. What was done was done.

Michael had gone along to give testimony and reported later that Marsh spent the next four hours pleading for mercy on behalf of Tom and Sean and filling out forms. They came to him and said they were sorry, he told the assistant D.A. They were willing to make restitution. They should be given another chance. He repeated it all to the judge hearing the case, with Tom and Sean sitting nearby. The judge dismissed the case after admonishing both boys that the best way to show their gratitude to him and to Mr. Greene was never to show up in his courtroom again.

"Marsh was amazing. He got them off. The gray-haired WASP in the wingtips fixed it with the gray-haired WASP in the black robes," said Michael, back at home and in front of Marsh. The three of us chuckled at the exaggeration, but it sounded about right.

Life was also going our way in our smaller world at 29 West, as we adapted to existence as a full-time foursome.

"When Mom's happy, we're all happy," Michael said.

Apparently he was correct, for Mom was ecstatic, and we had few disagreements to deal with as a new family. Amazingly few, considering the ages of my kids. It helped that Marsh came from a long line of mild-mannered conflict avoiders. It was not in his nature to go looking for a fight. It drove him crazy, for instance, that neither of our teenagers would jump up from the dinner table and do the dishes. This was ingrained behavior in his family. His kids didn't need to be asked. But I hadn't done such training. My two not only had to be asked, they put up a fight.

"I have so much homework tonight. Can't Michael do the dishes?"

"I did the dishes last night. It's Jennifer's turn."

"We weren't even here for dinner. Why should we have to do the dishes?"

But Marsh kept quiet in front of them. So I had to decide whether mandatory nightly kitchen cleanup was to be a *new rule* in the family. And whether he was to back me up as a co-enforcer. (For the record, it became a *new suggestion*, with varying degrees of compliance.)

I didn't mind making the decisions about how to deal with the kids, and in fact, I even preferred it that way. The strategy of my retaining control over the raising of my children seemed smart and fair. I got to keep my job as the boss, a position I liked and the three of us were accustomed to. Marsh got to be the good guy, loved and appreciated for adding adventure and security to our lives. Jennifer and Michael got to stay in their comfort zone as they adapted to the newness of a two-parent home.

As for Marsh's adapting to the three of us in those early months, I don't know how much tongue biting or acquiescing he had to do. He didn't talk about it, then or later. Like I said, it was his nature to avoid conflict. Plus, he was a simple man who was happy. Maybe so happy that he found it easy to put up with things about us that might have displeased him.

Or perhaps Margo, the psychic I liked to visit, had him pegged. She smiled when I first mentioned his name, well before our marriage. "I see the words 'old soul' and 'wise joy,'" she said.

Whatever the reason, Marsh kept his opinions to himself, and our melding into a family was happening without trauma. Jennifer did her part to make it easy. She was an excellent student who required little supervision. And she and Marsh shared a sensibility that had them howling at each other's jokes and weeping unashamedly during sad movie scenes. Michael presented more of a challenge. The gutsiness and independence that make him successful as an adult caused us some grief during high school. He coupled mediocre grades with garden-variety crimes, like spread-eagling on the roof of a car being driven past the vice principal's window. We were always on him and were constantly throwing darts at the punishment wheel.

By the end of our first year together, however, Marsh had loosened up. He griped freely about the kids' not cleaning up the kitchen and whatever else bothered him.

"How come you kids make a fire most nights, but I'm the only one who ever hauls in wood from outside?" he asked on more than one occasion.

But often as not, he would add with mock seriousness, "It just makes me furious." He punched each word and followed up with a grin. I wish I had a dollar for every time he said it during our twenty years together, softening his position and saving us from tension.

I also relaxed my grip on the parenting reins. After a year, the kids could go to either of us for rulings. And they felt comfortable enough to use the time-honored tactic of playing us off each other:

"But Mom said it was okay."

"But Marsh said I could."

At work, I made notes in my Day-Timer of things I would ask Marsh to help me decide that night at home:

"J's going to a concert on a school night—bad precedent?"

"Car for M—rewarding poor performance?"

For many years, I had sat up late, worrying about

decisions such as these, hoping I was doing right by my kids, living with the loneliness of a single mother. I had yearned for the long conversations of two loving parents who never seem to tire of talking about their children. Now I had Marsh, and we were those parents. The relief was so immense, it could bring me to tears.

I suppose a professed feminist shouldn't feel, or admit to feeling, the relief of sharing her life with a man. You know—*I am woman, hear me roar,* and such. But I had done my share of roaring. I had roared myself hoarse. It was a good thing now to rest a bit, to lighten my load by dividing it with Marsh, to open up to him and allow myself to be vulnerable because I knew I could do so without losing his respect.

"I love your strength, and I love taking care of you," Marsh said.

Like I said, I had it made.

## "Remember the Sweet Things"

· his making a fire in the master bedroom fireplace, then bringing up snifters of Spanish brandy to celebrate our first night in our first house

• walking up our street together, cooling down after our early-morning run

• his routine every workday morning of making us coffee and a plate of fruit, doing up dishes, fixing himself a bag lunch, and coming back up the stairs to kiss me goodbye

• his building a wooden mailbox, after declaring the store selections not good enough for our fine old house

• after chewing him out for shrinking some of my cotton shirts while doing the laundry, his standing before the washing machine, pretending to read a label: "This one says 'Rub with fine sand, then pound on a rock.'"

• talking the problem out, as many times as it takes, feelings on the table, neither of us afraid; later, hugging each other to sleep

• shaving every night before coming to bed. "But only until our first anniversary," he says; counting down—"Only eight more weeks to go," he says; his ceremonial breaking of the razor the night before our anniversary

• our longest bike ride, fifty-three miles; his riding up on the sidewalk now and again, "So I can ride next to you."

• picnicking next to the Charles River before seeing *Man of La Mancha* at an open-air theater

• my running late for work; coming out to my car on a cold morning to find he'd turned on the heater, cleaned the ice off the windows, and shoveled out around it

• bringing me a bouquet of spring flowers for no particular reason

• his saying, "I'm going to have a read," meaning he'll read for one hour, then feel compelled to go make or fix something; on a single Saturday, he split firewood, made a picture frame, fixed the garbage disposal, and cooked Basque garlic soup for our supper

• cooking together for ten hours on two nights, prepping for our tapas party

• my nervousness about doing a four-day training course in Puerto Rico in Spanish; his tucking an encouraging note into my travel bag, for me to find at the San Juan hotel

· the letter he wrote to "my clothier" (a salesman at Anderson-Little) who was about to retire, thanking him for thirty years of exemplary service

· his concern for Michael's difficulty with algebra and helping him at night with homework; his talking to the algebra teacher and choking up while telling her, "My son thinks he isn't smart enough to do well."

· helping me make ginger cookies; his goofy running commentary on his "techniques" for rolling and flattening the dough, checking the window to make sure no one saw him being "unmanly"

· when I wasn't feeling well, bringing me soup and cocoa

· en route to a weekend in Vermont, stopping to buy cough syrup so he wouldn't keep me awake

· humoring his sister while sorting through their mother's things after her memorial service:

HE: "I'll take the cut-glass lamp."
SHE: "I'll take the dining room table, chairs, and
    hutch."

• Friday Night at the Movies: chatting about the workweek while fixing ourselves a nice dinner; eating in the dining room with candles and wine and the good dishes; settling into the sofa for a VCR movie and falling asleep halfway through, as usual

• giving Michael a gift of a carving knife and a sharpening stone

• all the kids and grandkids at our house for the holidays: Jeff's five, Jen's three, Lisa and Eddie, Jennifer and Michael; Marsh and I operating like a well-oiled machine, keeping us all fed, watered, and happy

• working on *St. Kilda* on spring weekends, scrubbing, sanding, and varnishing; our self-congratulatory chatting on the drive home after a productive day

• the Mother's Day dinner that he and Michael cooked for Marjorie and me

• his obvious steering of conversations so he can just happen to mention that "my daughter Jennifer has won a UMass Chancellor's Award"

• his pride in his grass: "The boys down at Village Lumber tell me it's never looked better."

• the usual weekend sailing finale: a harbor cruise in Newport, zigzagging through the moorings, admiring and critiquing the boats

• spending hours rewrapping my bike's handle grips; his answer to my thank-you: "Nothing pleases me more than doing something nice for you."

• gathering mussels together off the rocks in Cutty Hunk Harbor; teaching me his recipe for stuffed mussels, adding, "As always, it's all about the butter."

• getting home from his trip to Eastern Europe and recounting his frustration with delays on the last leg because "they cut into my time with my wife"

• getting out of a warm bed to turn down the heat (which he assumes is only *his* responsibility); as always, returning and saying with a grin as he climbs back into bed, "Here I am again."

• Ellen, calling from another room: "I need you to do something."
Marsh, closing his book and getting up from his chair: "Here I come. I'm ready. I'm psyched."

· his teaching Michael to use an ax and split cord-wood

· his response to his best friend's calling him pussy-whipped: "I know. I like it."

· his spending hours down in the dirt cellar, converting the in-house outhouse into a wine cellar; the first night after finishing it, saying, "I'll just step down to the cave and see if I have a red that's matured."

· the thrill of singing his favorite, Verdi's *Requiem*, with two other choruses at Symphony Hall in Boston

· on the drive up to ski in New Hampshire, the ritual of stopping for Friday night supper at the House of Pizza in Orange, N.H.; his always playing "Christmas at the Lucky Lady Lounge" on the jukebox

· sailing to Block Island on an exquisite October Saturday; watching him trim a sail and filing the image in my memory bank

· passing out while giving blood during a Red Cross drive; happens often and embarrasses him, but doesn't stop him from giving every six months

· his missing Jennifer during her week in London, as evidenced by comments out of the blue: "I bet Jen's gotten her first good night's sleep tonight." "Jen's probably at Westminster Abbey right now."

· the predictability of his returns from Sunday morning tennis, Wednesday evening golf, and Saturday morning skiing: arriving home at the expected time, coming in the back door, and calling out, sitcom style, "Hi, honey, I'm home."

· his being a gracious loser at board games, but a really bad winner, especially at Trivial Pursuit; grinning his crinkly-eyed grin, commenting on how well he thought he'd played, trying to goad the rest of us into one more round

· his sitting up, waiting for Michael to come home on his first night out with his brand-new driver's license

· coming home with a rose and a sweet note, after I'd told him about my hard time with my boss

· the Maine cruise: his skill in bringing us out of the fog and clear of the rocks into beautiful little harbors; going ashore for a morning run and to gather mussels off the rocks; evenings back aft watching other boats come in and anchor; slow dancing in the cockpit at midnight

• his first, immediate, and only reaction to my idea of quitting my job, i.e., our losing my income, and going back to school for English teacher certification: full support and genuine enthusiasm

# Chapter 4

## *Expats in Shanghai:*
### *1991–1993*

"HOW ABOUT CHINESE FOOD TONIGHT?" MARSH called and asked.

"Fine," I said.

"Well then, how about Chinese food every night for the next two years?" he asked.

That was how, in January of 1991, he introduced the idea of our living in Shanghai. Jamesbury had asked him to set up and run a joint venture with Shanghai Valve Company #7. Was he interested? Would his wife be interested?

Interested? In the chance of a lifetime? To experience China as expatriates, on a U.S. corporate salary, with enough time to really get to know the place? We were elated. The timing was good for us, too. Both kids would be attending UMass-Amherst the next year, Jennifer as a junior and Michael as a freshman. I had given notice at my job already, in preparation for teacher training; I could postpone the training until our return.

But negotiations were still ongoing. Jamesbury had called them off the previous year after the Tiananmen Square incident in which hundreds, perhaps thousands, of students had died. The Americans continued to feel wary. Now their Chinese partners had to reassure them that a repressive government, capable of killing its own, was safe to do business with. Marsh and a Jamesbury delegation made several trips to Shanghai, where city officials and Communist Party heads convinced them, and the principal players became better acquainted.

A Chinese delegation came to Worcester, too, and I was included in some of the meals and outings scheduled for their entertainment. More than anything else, the group of eight wished to see how Americans lived. So Marsh invited them for Sunday brunch at our house. I managed to make some spectacularly wrong menu selections and served quiche, salad, and cookies to people who disliked cheese, didn't eat raw vegetables, and never picked up food with their fingers. But it didn't seem to matter. This was most people's first trip to the United States, and they wanted to try everything. They laughed at each other reaching for the cookies and accepted our offer to walk around the house, take a look at anything of interest, and ask questions. The garbage disposal and the spice rack seemed to impress them the most.

Marsh's future partner, Xiao Li, was there that Sunday. A few years later, over dinner at his apartment in Shanghai, he brought up that day.

"Some people wondered why a 'big potato' like Marsh chose to live in such an old house," Xiao Li said. Old, as opposed to historical or noteworthy. It's all relative, I suppose—if your country dates back to the dawn of history, a two-hundred-year-old house might not do much for you.

Xiao Li's observation reminded me of a conversation I had with a couple of young Chinese engineers, back in Shanghai after a ten-city U.S. tour that included New York, Washington, D.C., Chicago, and San Francisco.

"So which city did you think was the most beautiful?" I asked.

They needed no time to consider their answer. "Las Vegas!" they said.

Six months before our departure, Marsh and I began preparing ourselves in earnest for the two years in China. First we each took a month of intensive Mandarin Chinese classes. Then we plunged into logistics. Marsh wrote up and negotiated his salary and benefits package. It included hardship pay, a quarterly all-expense-paid vacation for two, and an annual monthlong home leave. We found a live-in caretaker for the house. We sorted and packed our things, assigning them colored dots—a green dot for Marsh and Ellen in China, a red dot for

Michael and Jennifer at UMass, a yellow dot for storage in our attic.

Then there were the blue dots. They were for Marsh only. He would spend the first four months in Shanghai by himself, the separation made more tolerable by a month of home leave at the halfway point. I would be staying in the U.S. until Michael graduated from high school and left for Air Force National Guard basic training in Texas. I would also be helping to move my mother, terminally ill with ALS, into a nursing home in Wisconsin.

"Don't help me pack," Marsh said. "It will only upset you." I proved him right by breaking down when I saw his boxes next to the front door, ready for pickup.

His last weekend before leaving, we were surrounded by family. Both of us fought for control throughout those two days, but at night in bed, we cried as we clung to each other and tortured ourselves with second-guessing.

"I know we can do this," I said. "But is it the right thing to do to ourselves? Or to the kids? Or to my mother?"

"And am I doing what I have always done—put my job before my family?" Marsh asked.

On Monday, our throats were tight during a silent ride to Boston's Logan Airport. We parked, and I walked with him as far as the screening gate. "I can't stand this," he said. "Let's just say goodbye quickly and go, without looking back." I agreed. We kissed hurriedly and then turned and walked away. But we couldn't do it. Both of us wheeled around for one last look, then returned to each other's arms for a final silent embrace.

The separation was as painful as we had anticipated. Marsh was living in a city of eight million people, with no one there to confide in. I was back in the familiar routine of a lonely single parent: go to work, eat a quiet dinner at home, get to bed early. We wrote long letters, sent gooey cards, talked on the phone, and soldiered through the first two months.

Marsh's home leave in June flew by, but fortunately so did the second two months of living apart. My brothers and I were busy with my mother as we emptied her apartment and settled her into a nursing home for what everyone expected would be the last six months of her life. Marsh scheduled a lot of road trips, taking long train rides to visit customers in backwater towns.

"I'm the only 'Round Eye' the kids have ever seen," he reported, using his translator's favorite moniker for Westerners. "They sidle up to me on the street and smile at me through their fingers. After a few seconds, they work up their nerve to touch my arm and then run away squealing."

By September, I was finally on my way to him, making the twenty-three-hour flight from Boston to Los Angeles to Tokyo to Hong Kong. Marsh met me in

Hong Kong, and we flew on to Shanghai together. Both of us were silly with excitement. We held hands and babbled between kisses throughout the flight. Marsh's company driver was waiting for us on arrival and drove us to our apartment at Shanghai Center in the heart of the city. He smiled at us in his rearview mirror as we gazed at each other and murmured over and over, in a kind of stupor.

"You're here; I can't believe it," Marsh said.

"I can't believe it; I'm here," I said.

I must have been groggy with jet lag, because it's the only explanation I have for my reaction to what Marsh said next.

"It's so disappointing that I have to leave this weekend for a ten-day trip," he said.

"Oh, no!" I said, and he moved on to another topic.

That was the extent of my protest at the time. Maybe I was overwhelmed by everything I must have been experiencing—elation, newness, disbelief. Regardless, he left on his trip and after two days alone, staring out our twenty-fourth-floor apartment window at the dirty air of Shanghai, it registered. "Have to"? What "have to"? He was the Big Deal Foreign General Manager. Who could force him to go anywhere? After an agonizing four months apart, how could he make me spend my first week alone, in a strange new country and apartment? More important, why was he willing to be away from me?

They were angry, rhetorical questions. I knew why. Marsh was in his dream job. Professionally, he was excited, needed, and important for the first time since he worked in Spain in the sixties. But I needed him, too. I was also dealing with some firsts. My youngest child had left the nest, and I now lived half a world away from him and his sister. My mother lay in a nursing home, dying of a horrible disease, and I couldn't be there to help her or my brothers. For over twenty years, I had had a career and an income of my own; now I had nothing to do and would have to ask my husband for money. The timing could not have been worse for Marsh to hand me another first: For the first time in our relationship, I had competition for his mind and heart. And his job had won.

Three days went by before he called.

"Hi, El. I miss you," he led off.

"Even if that's true, it's your own fault," I said.

There was silence on the line for a few seconds.

"I'm doing what I have to do, El. I'll be back in a week. You have to understand," he said.

"What I understand," I said, "is that I'm here by myself because the job came first. I'm hurt, I'm pissed off, and I want you to come home."

More silence on the line, followed by a too long explanation of how very important it was that he be there for a very important sale to a customer who was very important. So what did that make me? I started to cry.

"Okay. I'll try to get a train to Shanghai tomorrow," he said, his voice flat. "No promises, though."

He showed up two days later, needing a shave and a change of clothes.

"I'm sorry," he said that evening as we sat close to each other on the sofa in our living room. "It's the same mistake I made in my first marriage. I get caught up in work and expect my personal life to take care of itself. I appreciate your speaking up instead of silently resenting me."

And that was that. All's forgiven, end of discussion, we said.

But it wasn't the end of the discussion. For the duration of our first year in China, we remained out of sync with each other. Marsh was having the time of his life professionally, while I struggled to find meaningful work and things to do. And I wasn't alone. Some of the more experienced "following spouses" also found it hard to adjust to Shanghai. Some swore they suffered clinical depression, caused by low-grade lead poisoning from the polluted air (all the vehicles in China at that time used leaded gas, and coal dust in the air trapped the fumes). Others complained of chronic respiratory infections and skin rashes, also attributed to the city's bad air.

Mainly we wives just didn't have enough to do. Paid work was virtually impossible to find, even if you could wangle a visa. Not much call for volunteer work, either, in a Communist state with thousands of unemployed peasants pouring into the cities, looking for jobs. We had no homes or gardens to maintain—most of us lived in small, furnished, high-rise apartments reserved for foreigners.

Even recreation was hard to find. At that time, there were no theaters showing foreign movies, no golf courses, and no private clubs. Getting anyplace was complicated because we didn't have driver's licenses; foreigners were discouraged by their companies from driving because of penalties, up to and including deportation. Cars and drivers could be made available, but the scheduling and translating they required often weren't worth the hassle. I was spared a life of constant shopping when Marsh's partner, Xiao Li, found me a part-time job teaching conversational English at his alma mater, Tong Ji University. Not my idea of meaningful work, but I was forced to lower the bar from "meaningful" to "something to do."

In the meantime, our husbands were booked for the ego trips of their lives.

"My husband, the foreign management expert," said Elsie over lunch after aerobics one day. "He works six days a week and wouldn't mind making it seven. He is having a terrific time. His joint venture is way ahead of the profit plan, he has escaped a boring staff job back home in Stockholm, and he gets deference and respect from all his Chinese employees and customers."

Change Stockholm to Worcester, and it sounded like the Marsh Greene story. He was accomplishing big things, especially in the area he cared about the most—improving the quality of the valves coming out of the Shanghai factory. Because of him, Jamesbury became the second joint venture in China to earn ISO 9001 certification, a big stamp of approval in international manufacturing circles. He would go on to appear on television when the city of Shanghai awarded him their highest honor, the White Magnolia medal, for his contribution to their economic development.

And he was doing it in Chinese. He was the only expat general manager we knew of who could speak the language. Not that Marsh had any illusions about his status as a beginner. But he was improving, thanks to a tutor who came to the office three afternoons a week. Marsh always maintained, however, that his driver, Xiao Zhao, taught him the most. In his journal, he wrote about their conversations on the way to work:

"I get a lot of practice when I ride in the car alone with Xiao Zhao. Our conversation is wide-ranging and animated, even though I sound retarded and Xiao Zhao probably feels like the trainer of a circus bear. Listen to the English translation:

(First we take care of civilities and logistics.)

MWG: "Good morning. How are you?"

XZ: "Well, thank you. And you?"

MWG: "Well, thank you."

XZ: "You are going to the office (like every other day), right?"

MWG: "Right."

XZ: "And you are going home at five P.M., right?"

MWG: "Right."

(Now we can move on to other important topics.)

XZ: "The weather is very good today."

MWG: "Yes. It is sunny and warm."

XZ: "Are you too warm or too cold?"

MWG: "No. Just right."

XZ: "Tomorrow it might rain."

MWG: "That is too bad."

(Naturally much of our conversation revolves around cars and traffic.)

XZ: "Traffic is light today. In the morning, Yanan Street is not busy, but in the afternoon and evening it is busy."

MWG: "Yes."

XZ, on spotting a stretch limo: "A Cadillac. It is very beautiful."

MWG: "And very expensive."

XZ: "They are Taiwanese. They also have a Rolls-Royce."

MWG: "I saw it one time."

(Every third or fourth comment from Xiao
Zhao is followed by "Do you understand?"
[Ting de dong ma?] or by a stock phrase, like
"No problem" [Mei wenti] or a resigned "Not
much you can do about it" [Mei banfa].)

(We now discuss how business is going. Xiao
Zhao has a remarkable intelligence-gathering
network, so he knows everything that is
happening at the plant, and usually before I do.)

XZ: "I understand that visitors from [Company
ABC] are coming today."

MWG: "Yes. I worked on this visit for a long time."

XZ: "Will they bring a big order?"

MWG: "Maybe. Maybe not."

(At this point we roll into the plant. Xiao Zhao
turns off the air conditioner, unlocks the doors,
jumps out to open my door, and hands me my
briefcase, which always travels in the front seat.)

XZ: "See you at five P.M."

MWG: "See you at five P.M."

It has been another satisfying exchange. I am a
happy bear."

Marsh was having fun. And I was, too, only my
good times tended to fall mainly on Sunday. That was
the day we ran with "the Hash." Calling itself "a drink-

ing club with a running problem," the club consisted of anyone wanting to run through the alleyways of Shanghai for ten miles or so, chug beer from chamber pots afterward, and eat supper in hole-in-the-wall restaurants selected for their local color. We met our closest Shanghai friends at the Hash: Hennie from Holland, a World Bank consultant, laying out a Shanghai-wide transportation system; Michael and Ken from Australia, rerouting all of the city's sewage lines; and Guy from Britain, running a trans-Asia network of containerships. They, their wives, and most everyone who showed up on any given Sunday, were interesting, upbeat people; for me, being with them was therapeutic.

Formal company banquets and dinners with Xiao Li and his family often happened on Sunday night, too. It was low-key and comfortable at the Lis', who treated us like grandparents to their son, Yun Li. Their apartment was modest. We squeezed around a table in a room so small that people had to get up and move chairs in order to open the bathroom door.

The banquets were something else again—lavish affairs held in private hotel dining rooms decked out in red and gold flocked wallpaper and crystal chandeliers. Both Marsh and I gained ten pounds the first year in China, thanks to banquet hosts who risked losing face if they offered fewer than ten courses to their guests.

The banquets started simply enough. Dishes would

be brought out one at a time to each round table for eight and given a spin on the lazy Susan so everyone at the table could admire them. The exquisite food would keep our attention for a while: moist steamed river fish, bright green spinach and baby bok choy, plump glazed ginger shrimp. About half an hour into dinner, the toasting would begin. First, quiet reaches across the table to clink small glasses of beer or Heavenly Palace white wine. Then, people standing up, one by one, to offer florid toasts to others seated at the table. Soon the room was in motion as diners moved from table to table, outdoing each other with lavish toasts, sometimes silly, sometimes serious, but always insisting that drinks be drained, not sipped.

And then, as if someone had pressed a closing buzzer, the commotion would stop. Before people had a chance to make fools of themselves, the party was over. In a rosy glow of comradery, we would troop out to the cars waiting to take us home. Xiao Zhao invariably deposited us at our front steps no later than 10 P.M.

Jennifer and Michael joined us for the holidays that first year in China and attended several banquets, including one on Christmas Day that was billed as "A Western Holiday Extravaganza." And it was, in the sense that we still talk about it fifteen years later. It began on what we described as "a mistaken religious note." The venue was an auditorium in the middle of the city, and as we walked into the dimly lit, cavernous space, we were greeted by Madonna, on a giant screen set against a far wall, singing "Like a Virgin."

With no ado, a poker-faced young man in a black suit and white gloves ushered us to a long table, where we joined six people we didn't know, and dinner was served. The first course was ginger shrimp, a Shanghai favorite, but this time it was served cold, in a parfait glass, awash in pink tartar sauce and accompanied by a miniature bottle of Kahlúa. The second course included alphabet soup, definitely straight from a can. The third and main course consisted of dry turkey slices with a side of potato chips. Dessert was delivered by Santa, a skinny kid dressed in a baggy red union suit and straggly white Fu Manchu beard, who worked his way around the room, throwing tangerines and tiny chocolate footballs to us at our tables.

What the meal lacked, the after-dinner dancing made up for. It could have been 1920 on the Bund, in the ballroom of the Peace Hotel. Young and old Chinese dancers waltzed and quick-stepped by our table, backs straight, heads held high. They moved so gracefully and looked so elegant in suits and long dresses that we could almost disregard the music they were dancing to: big band arrangements of Christmas carols, including a heavy-on-the-sax waltz rendition of "Silent Night."

So much about that holiday became treasured memories for the four of us. We went to Beijing and acted like proper tourists as we visited the Forbidden City, the Qing Tombs, and the Great Wall, and smiled at the running commentary of Robert the Repeating Tour Guide (sample: "The stone camels represent the desert and the vastness of the emperor's reign. The vastness of the emperor's reign."). We went to Singapore and had dinner in a British club, but only after bare-ankled Marsh and Michael complied with the dress code and bought some socks from the maitre d'. We went to Bali and fell in love with Poppy's Cottages, the thatch-roofed huts for two, with outdoor showers and batik bedspreads, where tea and bananas waited on our porch every morning when we got up. It was a sad flight back to Shanghai for me, after seeing the kids off in Hong Kong.

Worse was yet to come. Three months later, out alone one morning for a run while Marsh was in Worcester, I misstepped on a speed bump in front of our apartment tower. My left knee turned, I felt something twist and snap, and I did a face plant onto the cement. I was able to pick myself up and hobble back to the elevator and our apartment. Two hours later, my knee had swollen and the pain was severe. Luckily, I had scheduled a car for that morning. I had bought a dragon's head cane as a gag gift for a friend's upcoming sixtieth birthday and used it now to get myself down to the waiting car. Xiao

Zhao, early as usual, took one look at me struggling to get down the front steps and hurried over to help.

"Leg . . . not good," I said.

That was enough for Xiao Zhao. He flashed on the hazard lights and we took off, blasting down Nanjing Lu, the busiest street in Shanghai, with the horn blaring nonstop. Headed for the "Foreigner's Clinic," it turned out, where Xiao Zhao got things moving quickly. He found a wheelchair and pushed me into a large reception area, where I gathered a crowd. Curious staff and visitors surrounded my chair as I stuffed my skirt into my crotch while two men in white smocks, presumably doctors, dug their fingers into my leg until I yelped at them to stop. Then it was down the hall for a quick X-ray and back to reception for the diagnosis. One of the doctors tore a page from a small desk calendar and sketched two bones with a jagged line running down one of them. He clenched his fists together and twisted them, as if wringing out a rag. The crowd nodded their heads and murmured their understanding.

On to a cast, with the reception room as good a place as any to slap one together. The White Coats dropped roll after roll of bandages in a bucket of graying water and slathered the sodden mess around my leg, splattering my chair and the floor with plaster of paris and coating my face, hair, and clothes, as they worked their way up from my toes to my groin. I looked like a mummyin-progress when Xiao Zhao finally wheeled me out to the car.

Others from the joint venture came to our apartment to help me the next four days, before Marsh's scheduled return. They arranged for a nearby restaurant to send up breakfast and lunch and for a cook to make dinner in the evening. They worried about my exposed toes and bought huge socks to fit over the cast. They declared the floor rugs a safety hazard and took them up. I was touched by all their acts of kindness. But the nights alone were long and painful, and I needed Marsh.

The worst, however, happened only a week later, and proved once again the adage that timing is everything. My mother died. Because of my leg, I couldn't go to her funeral. No airline could accommodate me in a full leg cast, and a U.S. doctor friend had strongly advised against my getting on a plane anyway. I prepared some remarks, which Michael read at her Mass, and my family called after the service and burial to console me.

I don't think Marsh could have counteracted all the sadness I felt that winter, and I didn't expect him to, either. Some diversions might have helped, though, and we didn't arrange for many. Marsh's contract allowed for a week's paid vacation every quarter, but we took only the holiday trip with the kids that first year in China.

"There's just too much going on right now," he would say when I brought up the idea of a getaway.

"That's a crock. There's always too much going on," I said. "You're not taking advantage of the great travel perk, and that's dumb. And unfair."

But I was the one being unfair. Nancy Reagan, someone I wasn't normally given to quoting, had it right when she described a good marriage as one in which the partners didn't expect a constant fifty-fifty arrangement.

"It's often ninety-ten," she said. "But if you're the ten, you know you will eventually get your chance to be the ninety."

I didn't have the generosity to let Marsh enjoy his turn at ninety, at least for the first year when he was adjusting to a new, higher level of responsibility.

"Do you resent my success?" he asked one night, when yet again he had come home to a sullen wife.

"No, I swear I don't. But I sure as hell am jealous of you," I said.

It took a brutal scare to snap me out of my selfishness and to help us correct our course. During Marsh's routine physical at the tag end of home leave in June, a doctor saw an elevated PSA score. Not much elevated, but enough to warrant a biopsy, he thought. It was a Thursday afternoon. Marsh had already left for China, with a scheduled stop in Austin to visit his daughters and their families. On hearing the news, daughter Lisa, a respected Austin nurse-practitioner, pulled some big strings and got him in the next day for the biopsy, with results promised for Monday.

It was an agonizing weekend for me in Westborough, waiting for Marsh's call from Austin. When the phone rang late Monday morning, I grabbed it after the first ring. It was Marsh. "El," he said, then stopped talking. I heard a muffled sob before he continued. "It's cancer, El."

Lisa, Marsh, and I moved quickly. Marsh would fly back to Massachusetts immediately. I would get on the phone and make appointments. Thanks again to old friends with connections, a Worcester-area oncologist, radiologist, and surgeon arranged to see him within the next three days.

Marsh and I handled crises in the same way. We hyperfocused on data gathering, analyzed the information quickly, and made a decision, with few or no changes of mind. This crisis was no different. We had cancer. We had three options: radiate, operate, or do nothing. Both the radiologist and the surgeon made their case for the superiority of their method. With either method, Marsh ran the risk of the same negative side effects— at least a 25 percent chance of nerve damage causing permanent incontinence or impotence. The oncologist reviewed the pluses and minuses of choosing neither method.

"Having one of the side effects terrifies me almost as

much as dying of cancer," Marsh said. I agreed, and we were only half kidding.

After long, candid phone conversations with Lisa, we opted for surgery. And once we made the decision, a kind of resigned calm came over both of us. We seemed attuned to each other more strongly than ever, as if words were no longer necessary now that we had agreed on what was to be done. As if simply holding hands, and we never seemed to let go of each other's hand during that week of staring into our unforeseeable future, would be enough to make everything turn out all right. One of my entries to the Sweet Things list, which I wrote a few days before Marsh's surgery, reflects how grounded I felt:

"realizing that I do truly, madly, deeply love him, for better or for worse, even if I didn't really know so on December 23, 1987" (our wedding day)

Nevertheless, anyone who has stood in a hospital corridor outside a recovery room, watching the surgeon coming toward you, knows the fear I felt. For hours I had riveted my eyes on every stretcher coming out of the O.R., looking for the familiar gray hair and ruddy face. Now it came down to the doctor standing before me, opening his mouth to speak. The news was good. Everything had gone well; no negative side effects were expected. Marsh was stable and resting comfortably.

His recuperation time passed quickly and smoothly. Marsh was a docile, uncomplaining patient whose positive disposition aided his recovery. I felt an intense tenderness for my dear partner, as he had for me when taking care of me earlier in the year. I couldn't do enough for him and loved it when he asked me to fetch things for him or to rub his back or to help him in and out of a chair. Our twice daily slow walks around the block, his leaning on my arm as we chatted and he got better, were a joy for me.

But Marsh wanted to get back to work, 100 percent ready or not. After a few weeks at home, we boarded a plane, bound for Shanghai and year two.

However, we were different people now. Marsh was a cancer survivor. For the first time, we faced up to the obvious truth that our time together was finite—whatever had a beginning also had an end, including us as a couple. This new gut feel for mortality did not make us fearful. It made us more adventurous and less reluctant to spend money on our own enjoyment.

"Come with me to Singapore," he suggested within days of our return to China. "I don't have to attend all the customer meetings. And let's treat ourselves and stay at Raffles."

We filled the fall of that second year with travel within

China. Together we took combined business and pleasure trips to Xi'an, Nanjing, Beijing, and Hainan. We spent a week on a Yangtze River boat, where we sat in deck chairs for hours, more fascinated by the thousands of peasants working along the river than the principal attraction, the Three Gorges. People washed babies, clothes, and themselves in the brown, silt-filled water. They unloaded coal from barges and hauled it in baskets that hung from poles across their shoulders. They bent over patches of plantings on riverbanks devoid of trees. "It's a big problem," the cruise social director told us. "Peasants cut down trees, even telephone poles, for firewood. The government has to pay them to leave the poles standing. Seven yuan a pole is the going monthly rate."

This was life for the 80 percent of China's 1.2 billion we never saw in the city. Town after town of a million or more inhabitants, living in soot-coated cement boxes scheduled to be inundated by a five-hundred-foot-high wall of water when the Three Gorges Dam opened. "They could sell it as 'architectural cleansing,'" Marsh said.

Our travel plans got bigger and better. Christmas in Mazatlán, where four of our kids joined us for a lovely tropical holiday. Chinese New Year in Hong Kong, watching fireworks over the harbor with 500,000 others. April in Japan, sitting among blossoming cherry trees in tranquil gardens. Home leave in June and sailing to Nantucket. Fall and winter trips to the monasteries of Tibet and the beaches of Phuket. Now *this* was expat living as we had fantasized it.

But obviously I couldn't expect a life of serial vacations, interrupted by Marsh's job. He enjoyed the job he was doing, and I had to let him do it. We agreed to a third year on his contract, and I went to work on my attitude toward Shanghai.

First I wrote a cookbook called *Made in China*, in which I shared recipes for familiar Western dishes, prepared with ingredients found in ordinary Chinese street markets, versus the pricey, imported Western food store. I improvised recipes for beef stew and strawberry pie, chicken Kiev and cucumber soup. If you needed a recipe to make mashed potatoes or a shopping list in Chinese to take along to the market, mine was the book for you. The People's Liberation Army Press printed several hundred copies, and I managed to sell them, a few by virtue of the printer's name alone.

Next I said yes to a long-standing request for a conversational English class at the joint venture. Xiao Li attended, as well as a dozen of the managers and support staff who made trips to Worcester. They were a good group. Twice a week, they showed up at 4 P.M. sharp, with homework in hand and a cheery "Hello, my teacher" on entering the room. We felt comfortable enough with each other after a while to take some risks, too. I conducted a session on cutlery, where the students struggled with knives and forks while cutting up tough pork chops and overbaked potatoes. Because they checked their egos at the door, we were able to have a lot of laughs in those classes. And I felt like part of the team, instead of just the "tai tai" (wife) warming a chair at banquets.

Marsh and I did something else together that both of us enjoyed. We shopped for antiques. "Mr. Wood," as the family nicknamed him, revered all things old and wooden; our cellar in Westborough was full of boards and beams he couldn't bear to throw away. So for Marsh, stepping into the warehouses stacked high with centuries-old furniture felt like being in church. In silent awe, he strolled down the rows of lacquered cabinets, high-backed chairs, and carved chests covered in dragons and phoenixes. He ran loving hands along them, not quite believing that he might be their next owner. We didn't buy much—only a couple of official's hat armchairs and a tea stand from the Qing dynasty era. For Marsh, the fun was in the fondling.

Never mind that the pieces we foreigners carried off might have been carried off once before. According to my dean at Tong Ji, what we ogled in the back-alley store was a mix of fakes made in "antique factories" around the city and genuine items that bore the red wax government seal of authenticity. Included among the latter were personal possessions stolen "in the name of the People" by fervent young Red Guards ransacking the homes of the elite during the Cultural Revolution. "They took everything," said the dean. "Furniture, dishes, rugs, even clothes."

The government later told the victimized that their things had been labeled and stored in state-owned warehouses. If they could provide proof of ownership, they could get them back. This was either impossible, or made impossible, for those who tried. Most people resigned themselves to their loss. "Mei banfa," said the dean.

I could understand this grudging acceptance. In China I had learned to accept and live with less than what I truly wanted. However, I was more than ready to leave by the end of the third year. Both of us knew that Marsh would have happily stayed on for the two years remaining until he retired. He was flying higher than ever, with the Shanghai factory considered the jewel in Jamesbury's crown. A despondent Xiao Li asked him to reconsider leaving, citing their personal friendship and how far Marsh had taken the company, with so much further still to go. "He had tears in his eyes when he asked me to stay," Marsh said, "and I had tears in mine when I said no."

"Ellen and I operate as an equal partnership," Marsh told him. "It's her turn now."

The fact that he meant it didn't make our departure any less wrenching for Marsh. As with the first year in Shanghai, the last found us out of sync. I was delighted to be leaving China; Marsh was despondent to be going home. For me, the next two years promised excitement and change as I finished teacher training and launched a career in U.S. public education. For Marsh, they promised a comedown and boredom as he returned to on-the-job obscurity, left to coast into retirement. Which is exactly how it turned out for him. Jamesbury had been bought and sold twice in the past nine years, the last time by a giant Finnish conglomerate with headquarters in Helsinki. As a minor player, little Jamesbury received scant attention from the corporate office; a sixty-three-year-old American employee, returning from an overseas assignment, could expect to receive even less.

Our last month in Shanghai was overwhelming. People swamped us with affection as they threw parties and came to our apartment for prearranged goodbye visits. A delegation of my students from Tong Ji University, friends from the Hash, Marsh's Mandarin tutor, our housekeeper and her husband, our neighbors in the apartment complex—all offered their best wishes and told us how much we'd be missed.

Jamesbury people touched us the most. The sales force often said, while toasting him at banquets, that they owed their personal success to Marsh's patient coaching.

Now, as a special goodbye gift, they pooled their annual bonus money to buy him a thirteenth-century ceramic vase, which they hand-carried from Nanjing and presented to him in our living room. Xiao Li gave us a gift of twelve place settings of china in a pattern he had seen me admire, and hosted four banquets in our favorite venues around town, with Communist Party officials, customers, suppliers, and everyone in his family invited to come to dinner and say goodbye.

The final farewell banquet included the Jamesbury "family" only and was held in the factory cafeteria, where, Monday through Friday, Marsh had eaten a hot meal prepared by the company cooks. They asked for the chance to do so one last time and had prepped for days. All three hundred fifty employees attended that evening, and both Marsh and I had been asked to speak. Knowing he would choke up while giving his speech, Marsh arranged for his interpreter, Dong Lan, to read it while he recited the Gettysburg Address. Dong Lan had tears in her eyes as she stood beside him and spoke the heartfelt words of his goodbye.

Sadness at the likelihood of never seeing most of these people again had tempered my elation about leaving. Guilt had as well. I hadn't even considered the option of remaining in Shanghai so Marsh could go out on a high note professionally, the guilt exacerbated by his never suggesting it to me, either. Both of us kept journals during the China years, and I have pored over them in search of trial balloons he might have floated about staying on. But I find none, and don't recall his ever bringing it up, much less trying to sell me on the idea.

Marsh's leaving without complaint was his most selfless act and the consummate sweet thing. I should have acknowledged this, I confess to you now, both out loud to him and in writing on my list, in order to give him the recognition he deserved.

## *"Remember the Sweet Things"*

• entertaining Michael and me after his first week of Mandarin Chinese lessons: "Do you want to hear me say 'two yellow buses'?" "Now I'm going to say 'three red pencils.'"

• his calling from the new apartment in Shanghai and pretending to quiet down "the girls" there with him

• his description of April's opening ceremonies at the plant: the twenty-piece band welcoming him with a spirited rendition of "an old American favorite" ("Jingle

Bells"); his giving a four-line speech in Chinese and the crowd's laughing and applauding the effort

• on the phone, defending the merits of our different countdown methods; he prefers chalking it off day by day, I like the bigness of one-quarter over, one-third over, etc.

• the excitement of his home leave after two months and meeting him at Logan; people smiling at a sixty-year-old man and a forty-five-year-old woman flying into each other's arms and kissing with abandon

• the second separation being easier because of its finality and our learning to alternate moods—if he's down, I do cheery; if I'm crying, he consoles

• his partner Xiao Li's concerned reaction to my baking and air mailing a big batch of his favorite oatmeal cookies: "Marsh, tell Ellen not to worry about your health. My brother-in-law can bring you oats from Hong Kong."

• reuniting for good in Hong Kong, he at the bottom of a long runway with an armload of roses and waving wildly

• our first walk to the neighborhood open-air produce market; buying "leaves" (the only word we understood) that we didn't know how to cook

• his leading the way on my first bike ride, weaving
a path among thousands of riders on one of the busiest
streets in Shanghai

• our returning from Xi'an on China Air; a grinning Xiao Zhao waiting for us with the Crown Toyota
parked on the tarmac, white gloves on, holding the door
open for us "big potatoes"; he'd pulled some strings, he
said, very pleased with himself

• with Jennifer and Michael, slipping and sliding
along the Great Wall in an ice storm; being drilled be-
forehand by our tour guide on the Principle of Security,
i.e., Be back to the bus on time, and the Principle of
Satisfaction, i.e., Be back to the bus on time so everyone
will be happy.

• a vacation in Bali; Jennifer's disappointment at not
finding a nice shell on the beach; his buying one and
planting it for her to "find"

• "China Marsh, the Negotiator" on his successful
buy at the beach in Bali: "That six-year-old drove a hard

bargain. But I managed to get the 1,200 rupia straw hat for 1,200 rupia."

• the surprise birthday party for his sixtieth with many new friends crammed into our one-bedroom apartment, there to wish him well

• my breaking my leg while he's in the U.S.; his traveling for two days straight, trying to get back to Shanghai; coming in our apartment door exhausted and disheveled but with the usual goofy "Hi, honey, I'm home."

• Marsh the Caregiver: every morning for a week, giving me a sponge bath, making me breakfast, getting me settled in a comfortable chair with my leg propped up and a thermos of coffee within reach; his going to work and returning at 1 P.M. to make lunch and stay with me the rest of the day

• ELLEN: "Could you please get me a beer?" (as
he settles into the sofa to watch a movie, after
making dinner and cleaning up)
MARSH: "Now, wasn't it you that I asked only a
few seconds ago, 'Do you want anything else?'
To which you said no and gave me a beatific

smile." (as he smiled and got up to go to the refrigerator)

ELLEN: "I never smile beatifically."

• my being particularly crabby one Sunday morning and his deciding to cheer me up with eggs Benedict: riding his bike over to the Hilton and wrangling some Canadian bacon from their kitchen; a lot of pan clanking and bellowing "son-of-a-whore" coming from the kitchen; serving with mock fanfare and congratulating himself on "the perfect garnish for some needed color" (a lettuce leaf sticking out of the hollandaise sauce)

• his rolling out wonton skins, singing "Bringing in the Sheaves" in garbled Chinese

• packing but not wearing his tuxedo at his daughter's wedding because he didn't want to draw attention away from the more casually dressed groom

• on home leave, down in the dirt cellar, getting ready to paint the dining room together; his waving the good Purdy brush in my face and teasing, "You can't use this one. You can look at it, but you can never ever touch it."

· a leisurely afternoon, anchored off Block Island, reading our books, enjoying one of his Bloody Marys, taking a swim and a nap together

· witnessing the warm reception he gets from his Chinese staff at banquets, where they come to our table and raise their little cups of Heavenly Palace wine in toast after toast

· my feeling vaguely out of sorts when he's out of town on a trip; keeping a list of inconsequential things to remember to share with him when he gets home

· the unspoken Christmas crèche game he plays with the housekeeper: She rearranges the crèche every time she comes to clean, moving the animals out of the stable and the Three Kings in; he puts them back in biblical order; she moves them again to what she considers their rightful places

· for our fifth anniversary (wood), commissioning for me a hand-carved mahogany recipe box, monogrammed and covered with Chinese symbols for health and happiness

· having a beer in a park in Osaka; some Japanese students asking if we'd like to share their cooler of drinks (and let them practice their English?). "You movie star?" one of them asks. "Look like Paul Newman."

* the affection of Marsh and Xiao Li for each other; more than just business partners, they like spending time together, and their joint venture is a Shanghai success story

* running with the Hash and getting lost in the maze of narrow alleyways, the locals standing in their doorways cheering us on as we run by

* his taking me along on business trips; in one year alone, the job and vacations taking us to Xiamen, Nanjing, Hong Kong, Singapore, Taiwan, Japan, Tibet, and Thailand

* in a Tibetan monastery, a little boy monk, maybe ten years old, giving him a high five and a sweet smile; his responding with a hand-slapping game of "gotcha"; soon surrounded by little monks wanting to play

* on the Three Gorges river cruise: breakfast at 8 A.M. sharp, we're told. At 7:45, music is piped into our cabin. At 7:50, the announcement that breakfast is ready. At 7:55, housekeeping enters without knocking and states, "Time to clean room." His smiling and saying, "A taut ship is a happy ship."

• visiting an important Canadian customer; at the Calgary Stampede, two dishy blond twentysomethings asking him to line dance

• the hours we spend writing and rewriting "Double Happiness: A Joint Venture Adventure," getting it ready for Christmas gift giving to our family

• the incredible last two weeks in Shanghai, feted every night with dinner parties and gifts, including an old chipped "piss pot" from the Hash

• his surprise of first-class seats for the final flight home; our subdued mood as he closed out the best job he'd ever had

# Chapter 5

## Crossing the Pacific: 1994–1996

WITHIN A YEAR OF REENTRY INTO LIFE IN THE U.S., we began planning to leave again. While still in China, Marsh and I toyed with the idea of sailing *St. Kilda* around the world. We would pump ourselves up, looking at *Cruising World* magazine photos of boats anchored off idyllic beaches, and ask, "Why not?" Really, why not, now that Marsh had only a few months until retirement and Michael was about to graduate from UMass. I had finished student teaching but hadn't landed a job yet. The timing seemed perfect for a circumnavigation.

If I had to name one thing that made Marsh and me compatible partners, it would be the "why not" attitude we shared. "Would you like to drive into Boston for dinner this weekend?" "How about we go see my mother tomorrow night?" "What do you say we raise the roof and add a sleeping loft for the grandkids?" The first reaction, his and mine, would be a knee-jerk "Sure, why not?" Later, after more discussion, we might change our minds. Initially, however, we could count on each other's enthusiastic reception of an idea. It helped that our tastes were similarly modest, so the ideas usually didn't call for big outlays of cash. Still, the dependable positive response was no small thing. Both of us were already self-confident and not averse to taking risks. Now, feeding off each other, we generated more ideas and considered bigger adventures.

This circumnavigation idea called for more than adventurous spirits, however. Sailboat live-aboards can get by on a shoestring budget, experienced cruisers told us, but it would take thousands of dollars to outfit *St. Kilda* for her voyage of a lifetime. As my sister-in-law, Teri, wryly noted, "I could make a round-the-world trip staying in Marriott luxury suites for less than you guys are willing to spend on a forty-foot boat." We realized right away that we needed boat partners to share the adventure and the expense. Thankfully, our good friends and sailmates, Kevin and Marge, required no convincing. They would take sabbaticals from their respective teaching and technical writing jobs and sign on for the first year of passage-making.

But before taking off, we had two important matters to attend to. The first was "my" Jennifer's June wedding. She had moved to San Francisco, landed a nice job at an advertising agency, and met Patrick, an engineer and son of Dubliners. We had been introduced the year before and hit it off with Pat immediately. They would be married by Jonathan, the same man who married Marsh and me seven years earlier, and the reception would be held at our home. As with our own wedding, we spent weekends and evenings buffing up the place, putting a fresh coat of paint on every surface, refinishing all the pine floors, and filling empty spots in the garden, this time with pink and white begonias, petunias, and impatiens.

Ireland played Italy in a World Cup match in New York City in June that year. The wedding date was set to accommodate the soccer-crazy Irish relatives who talked about coming to the States that weekend for the match. Lucky for us, we could blame it on them that Jennifer's wedding fell on the hottest June weekend ever on record in Massachusetts.

No one suffered on Friday, aboard sailboats in the middle of Narragansett Bay. Everyone under thirty was put aboard *St. Kilda,* with Kevin at the helm and beer and jug wine on ice. The older set went out with a better bar and Marsh's oldest friend, Bill, on his boat, *Cherish.* There was just enough of an early-evening breeze for *St. Kilda* and *Cherish* to put up sail and glide past the elegant old summer homes lining the bay, before rafting up together for the seafood and salads we brought along in coolers.

Saturday was another story. By midafternoon, the temperature reached 99 degrees and leaves hung limp in the trees. Jennifer had chosen wisely when she selected a short, sleeveless silk dress from the 1920s that she found in a vintage dress shop in San Francisco. But her bouquet was wilting before our eyes as Marsh walked her down the aisle of First Church of Framingham.

Jonathan admonished the assembled to concentrate on the importance of the occasion and not their own discomfort, which would be relieved in approximately twenty-five minutes. The suffering of the Irish soccer fans was particularly acute, for the Ireland-Italy match had begun as they took their seats in the church.

The service ended in the promised amount of time, the receiving line and picture taking dispatched "in a seamanlike fashion," as Marsh was fond of saying, and the fans dove for their cars. By the time he and I arrived back at the house, they had circled the TV, drinks in hand, and were howling their approval as Ireland scored the first goal of the match and went on to win, 1–0. Their good mood set the tone for the rest of the evening, which ended with all the guests encircling Jennifer and Pat, hooking arms, and drowning out Roy Rogers and Dale Evans in a raucous rendition of "Happy Trails to You."

The second matter requiring our attention was the sale of our now buffed-up house. Better to be out from under house upkeep while at sea, we figured, especially given our fuzzy plan to leave snow country at some point after Marsh retired. And we thought it signaled our commitment to living on a boat. So, after one last summer in the beloved old place, we put it on the market. It sold in two months.

Walking away from 29 West Street would have caused us more pain without the excitement of the upcoming voyage. We occupied ourselves for months with all the things we had to do to prepare *St. Kilda* and crew. The boat needed new everything: new sails, new dinghy, new dinghy engine, new life raft, new lifelines, new sheets, new anchor. It needed better safety gear, like an EPIRB (emergency position-indicating radio beacon), a GPS (global positioning system), a self-steering device, a desalinator, and a complete engine overhaul. And for us, all affordable thanks to the sale of 29 West.

The gear and preventive maintenance were must-haves, at least if you planned a stop in New Zealand, as we did, to wait out hurricane season. The Kiwis had passed maritime laws recently that forbade a boat's leaving their waters without a full inspection and the safety gear they deemed necessary. Apparently they were tired of their taxpayers having to foot the bill for expensive rescues at sea of crippled, ill-equipped vessels. Fair enough for a nation with ten times more sheep than people.

We also needed charts. Marsh was a stickler about charts. Other cruisers relied on local knowledge they picked up along the way or on their own experience, but Marsh wouldn't risk us or the boat. For him, it was simple—no chart, no go. From a planning perspective, this meant the four of us had to agree many months in advance on which islands, and which sections of those islands, we wanted to visit. Charts were not usually available once under way, and mailing them to a boat en route was notoriously unreliable. In some instances, the advance planning was easy—when you sail to Tahiti, you put in at Papeete, the only allowable place to register your entry. In other instances, you had homework to do—when you sail to the Marquesas, you could register at Nuku Hiva or Hiva Oa. Which would it be?

When it came to using the charts, I was a weak link. I didn't know how to read them or how to plot a course on them. So I signed up for back-to-back navigation courses taught by the U.S. Coast Guard. I also got serious about tying knots. Over every winter I seemed to forget the knots I could tie the previous summer. I bought an Eddie Bauer knot book and practiced each one over and over until I could tie a bowline with my eyes closed and a double clove hitch in three seconds.

Provisioning I could handle, no problem; cooking

and menu planning were my forte. The rule of thumb for passage-making was enough food for the expected number of days out, plus an extra 50 percent in case of emergency or slow going because of no wind. So, for example, a two-week passage for the four of us meant provisions for two hundred fifty-two meals. Plus snacks for night watches, drinks throughout the day, and wine for that one and only glass we planned to savor each night before dinner. All made more challenging by the boat's lack of a refrigerator.

First I perused recipes and cookbooks, in search of dishes where canned meat and vegetables could substitute for fresh. I picked the ones with the fewest ingredients and the easiest execution; I had drained the optional can of olives before, struggling to stay upright in a rough seaway, while onions burned in the skillet and lunch worked its way up my throat. Then I tested each recipe and served it to Marsh. If he liked it, I wrote a small *m* above its name, which identified it as a keeper.

The final step called for assembling the meals into a plan. I prepared three breakfast, lunch, dinner, and snack plans for fourteen days. A plan consisted of the menu for each day, the recipes for each dish, and the ingredients written on a shopping list we could carry ashore. I gave myself two guidelines—no repeats on the dinner menus within the two weeks, and no ingredients difficult to find outside the United States, like peanut butter or cornmeal. I wrote everything on five-by-seven cards and categorized the cards in a waterproof accordion file.

I also inventoried the contents of all the storage lockers on the boat, arranged things in labeled bins, and wrote up a log. If we needed grommets, we could look them up in the log and find them in the forward head, port side, top shelf, bin 2, or as listed in the log "FH-P-T-2." I can't make the claim that the log ever saved our bacon. But it cut down on some of the frustration under way, when seas were heavy and nerves already frayed, and we were spared a fumble through lockers looking for duct tape or Band-Aids or a can of tomatoes.

Navigation, knots, and provisioning were fun. Learning Morse code was not. But someone had to pass the code test in order for *St. Kilda* to have ham radio access in case of an emergency. So Marsh and I volunteered to try. We made it a competition and listened separately to practice tapes recorded by an effusive ham operator named Gordo. We renamed the reading nook off the kitchen "the code shack" and hunkered down in it for hours, listening to Gordo and filling notebooks with dots and dashes.

But we weren't getting it. Neither one of us could take down much more than five words a minute, and we needed thirteen to get the radio license. Marsh told me about a corpsman he knew in the Navy who could transcribe a hundred words a minute and walk away to get himself a cup of coffee while doing it. Hearing about him didn't help. Our frustration mounted. I heard Marsh practicing an exercise one Saturday, playing one section of tape over and over. With each rewind, Gordo chided, "Don't throw that pen down! Come on! You can do it!" I heard the ping of a pen bouncing off the cassette player and Marsh shouting, "A pox on your house, Gordo!"

We signed ourselves up for the test anyway, on the off chance that one of us would get lucky. I was prepared to cheat. I brought along a forged doctor's note, attesting to my dyslexia, which meant a dispensation and permission to pass at five words per minute. But the ghost of Gordo was with me that day. I took code as miserably as ever, but guessed enough right answers to questions about the transcribed message that I passed fair and square.

By late August, the four of us and *St. Kilda* were ready. We headed out from Jamestown, Rhode Island, our home port, bound offshore for Norfolk, Virginia, in seas that by afternoon had grown to twenty-five feet. *St. Kilda* slid up and down the troughs of water like the tough North Sea veteran she was, and the impressive maiden voyage left us soggy but confident, in her and in ourselves. We reached our final destination for that leg, Beaufort, North Carolina, and left her there for a few months, while we finalized the house sale and packed up our belongings one more time.

Marsh and I came back after Christmas to go it alone the next leg, down the Intracoastal Waterway to Fort Lauderdale, Florida. "Doing the Ditch," boaters called it.

It was cold that January on the coast of North Carolina. "*Cruising World* magazine never shows photos of the crew in mittens," I said as we scraped ice from the windscreen and pitched snow from the decks. But that was us every morning the first week on board. The raw wind off the water went straight to the bone, and we kept our mugs filled with steaming coffee and soup. We had no hot water in the head, so we showered in marinas along the way. We had no space heater, so we slept in the galley with the oven door propped open, going to bed and getting up with the sun.

Marsh held me close in bed under a mound of covers. "I love this," he said. So did I.

We motored down the Intracoastal at a leisurely pace of six knots, trying to stay in the middle of the channel. *St. Kilda* drew five feet and touched bottom often enough to make us less panicky when we eventually did go aground. Nothing serious—no leaning on our side, waiting hours for high tide. It was embarrassing, though, when another boat passed and its crew barely suppressed the schadenfreude in their concerned looks.

Payback, we figured, for all the times in home waters that we smirked at others as they lunged for the mooring ball and missed, or crash-landed at the fueling dock and upended their crewmates.

For two weeks, we poked along and admired the low country houses lining the waterway, the owners' boats tied to docks and bobbing out front. How about a home on the ICW, we said, already scheming and dreaming about life after this trip. We could sit on our porch and watch the yachts glide by as they made their way as far north as Maine in the summer and as far south as Florida in the winter. The nearby towns had their charm, too—the front porches of Belhaven, the Victorians of Brunswick, the squares of Savannah. Each night, we put into a new town and a different slip, and jumped off for a meal and a reconnoitering of the area.

Fort Lauderdale marked the end of the waterway for us. The few days we planned to spend there dragged into a few weeks. A front took its time passing through, and we listened to the radio for the all-clear from the Coast Guard before crossing east to Bimini in the Bahamas. After a month of island-hopping and lazy days of snorkeling and swimming, we picked up again with Kevin and Marge, who flew into Georgetown in the Exuma Cays to meet us. We were excited, anxious to test our mettle, eager for the real passage-making to begin.

Enough of this day-tripping from one luxury marina to another, sails rarely pulled out of their bags.

We set sail for the Windward Passage, between Cuba and Haiti, en route to Panama. This leg would take nine days, with no sight of land—our first serious test as cruisers. We were ready.

But *St. Kilda* was not. On the second day, Marsh and Kevin discovered an alternator problem. The batteries were overcharging, which meant they would eventually burn out and leave us without power. Power needed for running lights at night, if nothing else, to announce our presence to other vessels. We had to stop and find a mechanic.

Marsh wondered if the U.S. Navy would accept us at Guantánamo. But what if there were no facilities for civilian boat repairs there and we had bypassed other options? We decided not to take a chance. Instead, we ducked into Matthew Town, on Great Inagua Island, the closest stop on our course heading. We found out on arrival that it was also a mining camp for the Morton Salt Company, which meant mechanics on their payroll. We asked around and soon met a Bahamian who said he could fix the problem.

He couldn't. He did manage to cobble together a fix that proved sufficient to get us under way and to our destination in Panama, but the fix was not permanent. This would be our experience across the Pacific as mechanics throughout the archipelagos took a crack at our problems: the noncharging alternator, the nonreading gauges, the nonworking bilge pump. Always the mechanic or electrician shook Marsh's hand and declared the problem solved. Always we limped into the next port and looked for another.

Once under way from Inagua, we settled into some fixed routines. We divided the night into four-hour watches, which meant each of us had the fourth night off. Marge and I cooked in two-day shifts. Both of us preferred it that way, plus it made for better use of leftovers. Marsh handled most of the navigation; he took star sightings, plotted courses, and tinkered with the GPS. He and Kevin did most of the sail handling. They repeatedly tweaked the sheets and adjusted the self-steering vane, more for something to do than any real need, I thought a few times. The four of us read for hours from the scores of books that lined our cabin walls, and wrote long letters to our families and trip reports for the *Worcester Telegram and Gazette,* which printed them as an ongoing feature.

Meals were the highlight of each day. Even without refrigeration, Marge and I sent up some fine plates of food from that galley, at least according to four people resigned to high carbohydrates and produce from cans. Dinner fare might be chicken "stroganoff" with rice and a side of stewed tomatoes, or rigatoni with green beans and tuna, plus a cup of fruit cocktail. Our concoctions often included eggs, onions, or cabbage. Those three fresh foods lasted for weeks on a boat, if you remembered to turn the eggs every other day and to peel the leaves of a cabbage instead of cutting into it.

We baked like Fanny Farmer, too. We made cookies and scones and lopsided cakes, when the boat heeled and took the cake batter with it. We put bread dough on deck to rise in the sun and baked three or four loaves a week. For me, the piquant smell of the bread coming out of that oven ranks as best-in-my-lifetime.

Marsh bragged about us to other cruisers in the anchorage who were sitting down night after night to spaghetti Bolognese and canned corned beef hash. "*St. Kilda* is the best eater in the fleet," he said.

Or if others asked us to join them for a meal on shore, he liked to use Paul Newman's retort to a question on temptation and women other than his wife: "Why should I go out for a hamburger when I have steak at home?"

However, I retract the statement that meals were the highlight of our day. A glass of cheap Chilean box wine was the highlight of our day. Every night we cracked open one of the forty boxes of Fray Leon tinto stowed under the forward berth. You could set your watch by our body language as we closed in on the five o'clock happy hour. Someone taking a nap would pop up from below. A reader of an interesting book would place it facedown and stand up for a big stretch. Marsh would stop his calculations at the chart table and return the parallel rule to its case. There would be small talk and casual glances at wristwatches for five minutes, then Kevin or Marsh would sound the hour with the ritual feigned surprise and rhetorical question.

"Well, look at that. It's five o'clock already. A sip of the grape anyone?"

We acknowledged that special occasions deserved celebration, meaning an extra ration of wine for all hands. The first and last days of a passage qualified as special. So did Bastille Day. And St. Swithin's Day. And the day we saw a bird. And the day we used up the last onion.

The nine days passed uneventfully on that first leg to Panama. Which made Marsh's reaction to it all the more shocking.

"I despised it, El," he said as we lay close in the forward berth, *St. Kilda* tied to a dock in Colón. I reached for his hand and felt the sweat on his palm as he confessed to me in the dark.

"The anxiety just ate away at me. I was always waiting for something to go wrong and worrying that we wouldn't be able to fix it," he said, sounding edgy and accusatory. "But the night watches were the worst. Alone in the cockpit, with nothing to do and nothing to distract me." He paused, as if to assure himself of what he would say next, and let out a heavy sigh before continuing. "Life is too short. El, I cannot go on with this," he said, his voice flat with failure.

He, the ex-Navy commander, the captain, the most experienced among us, wanted to abort the trip. The long-planned, much-proclaimed, savings-draining trip we had bragged about for a year to anyone who gave us an opening. The trip that had elated him only a few months before, in the ice and snow of North Carolina. Lying there in the dark, I felt punch-drunk from the body blows Marsh continued to deliver as he admitted to the nervousness and boredom he had felt since the Bahamas.

"I thought I'd get over it. And I hated to let you down," he said. "Or to have you think I was some kind of wimp, so afraid of going aground. And so nervous getting us in and out of anchorages." Interesting sights and ports of call had not compensated for the constant knot in his stomach while under way.

I tried to be empathetic. I rolled him on his side, rubbed his back, and mouthed some words about also becoming bored with long days on the water. But you can't fake empathy—you feel it or you don't. What I felt was shame, and it was written all over the face I now hid from him. He was a quitter. I would be called a quitter, too. People would cluck with understanding, but I knew what they would say behind our backs. They would blame it on me, too, no matter what he said. I could almost feel myself shriveling under hot waves of humiliation.

And of disappointment. A slow-burning disappointment, like molten lava, oozing its way down my body. All the preparation. All the anticipation. All the pride in what we were undertaking. Selling 29 West, Morse code, thousands of dollars, hundreds of hours, recipes, inventories, newspaper articles, bon voyage gifts, goodbye kisses. For what? We lay there for a while in silence, unable or unwilling to offer each other solace; I could hear the tears dropping on his pillow and dreaded breaking the sad news to Kevin and Marge in the morning.

"Never go to sleep angry with each other" is a bromide sometimes offered to newlyweds. It never worked for me. Nor made a lot of sense to me—is it reasonable to expect two tired people, under the influence of Morpheus and perhaps more, to come to a sensible, loving consensus? I preferred another old saying: "Things look better by light of day." Keeping my mouth shut and waiting until morning, or next week or next year, had been known to make me more fair-minded. As happened here, when I received the message sent to me overnight, special delivery.

"Your turn," it said. It was my turn, as it had been

Marsh's in Shanghai, to swallow the disappointment, to support my partner, and to act in the best interest of our marriage. You know, like we promised, for better or for worse.

Besides, early on in the planning process, we all had agreed that any one of the four of us could back out of the trip at any point, with no fear of recrimination. After all, none of us had experienced passage-making for long periods on a small boat. Kevin and Marge remembered that agreement and reacted accordingly the next morning when a dejected Marsh repeated what he had said to me. Their magnanimity humbled me. They understood, they said, and were sorry that Marsh was having a rough time of it.

"This should be an adventure, not an endurance test," said Kevin.

But what were we to do? Parked in a slip, waiting our turn to go through the Panama Canal, we laid out the options. Marsh and I could get off, and Kevin and Marge could continue for their promised year. We would figure out later how to get the boat back to Jamestown. Or the four of us could go back the way we had come but take some time to gunk-hole around the San Blas Islands off the eastern coast of Panama. Or go farther south to include the Caribbean islands off Venezuela's coast. Or pass through the Canal and head north to Mexico and California.

Or pass through the Canal and complete part of the trip as planned.

"Marsh, could you see your way to island-hopping across the Pacific?" asked Kevin, posing the same question I had thought of the night before. "Lots of stops that way. Marge and I could take the boat on from there. And we can work out the watch issue. Maybe shortening them from four hours to two or three."

Marsh didn't hesitate. He agreed to crossing the Pacific, and the rest of us smiled with relief. To all of us, it felt like a good compromise and the best choice. And in retrospect, we did make a sound decision. We managed to salvage the sexiest part of the voyage and to lighten Marsh's inevitable burden of guilt.

So *St. Kilda* passed through the Panama Canal, sandwiched between freighters and looking like a bathtub toy. We joined the parade of pleasure boats on the annual "coconut milk run," named for its steady winds, easy passages, and lovely tropical island destinations. The flotilla sailed downwind and west across the Southern Hemisphere from April to October, thus avoiding the cyclone season. While we rarely saw each other under way, we maintained regular radio contact with other boats and tended to arrive and depart from the same anchorages in batches. So we got to know each other.

"G'day there, Cap'n," called Bill, an Aussie boat-builder and part of our batch, leaning against his mast and watching us come in. "As usual your North Sea tub is the last one in."

The great-grandson of a woman sent out from Ireland for the crime of stealing her mistress's hair ribbon, Bill never tired of ragging on *St. Kilda* and all things British. Swapping stories with him and other captains over beers at yacht clubs along the route eased Marsh's anxiety. Most boats, like ours, needed repairs at most stops, and the captains had to keep an eye out for the corrosion caused by continuous chafe. Marsh liked to tell the story of his opening a box of cornflakes to find a pile of dust, the flakes pulverized by the constant shaking of the boat. Most captains also agreed with him that the best part of cruising wasn't the sailing, it was the stopping—stopping in exotic ports of call for a cold beer, a hot shower, and a long look around.

Our first taste of exotica after the Canal was Santa Cruz in the Galápagos. After a fourteen-day passage, Marsh and I scrambled to pack a bag, hopped in the dinghy, and checked into a boutique hotel for the duration of the stay. This became our modus operandi across the Pacific—to reward ourselves at every stop with clean, dry sheets and a bed that didn't sway.

We reveled in these simple luxuries in Santa Cruz and in the nightly "plato del dia" at Big David's three-table restaurant, set up a few blocks from the hotel on the side of a dirt road. His coconut langosta stew was our favorite. "This is, by far, the best meal I have ever eaten," said Marsh, his judgment perhaps impaired by his euphoria at being ashore.

I will spare you a travelogue and a description of tours and tortoises on the Galápagos. They seemed incidental to our main mission, anyway, which was to prepare ourselves and the boat for the longest passage of the voyage. Twenty-five days from the Galápagos to the Marquesas. The engine would be shut down, the gas to run it conserved for an emergency. The water would be rationed to a liter per day, meaning seawater sponge baths and clammy clothes. The Fray Leon tinto would be put to the test as we strove for contentment during three weeks at sea. This would be the Boston Marathon of passage-making.

The trip didn't live up to the hype, however. The engine wasn't needed because the southeast trade winds blew every day. A liter of water is enough when you bring along four hundred cans of juice. And mind-numbing boredom didn't occur because we learned how to suck an activity dry. I killed an afternoon, for instance, monogramming four dozen oatmeal cookies by counting out raisins and walnut pieces and arranging an exact number of each to form our initials.

Plus *St. Kilda* not only stayed problem free, she set her fastest pace to date, averaging one hundred fifty miles per day. As the sun came up on the twenty-fifth day, the four of us stood in the cockpit, gaping at the wall of algae-covered rock that announced the harbor of Hiva Oa and high-fiving ourselves for our accomplishment.

Hiva Oa, Moorea, Huahine, Tahiti, Bora-Bora—the island names of French Polynesia evoke images that matched their reality. Brown-skinned beauties with flowing black hair did indeed amble along streets lined with towering coconut palms and hibiscus bushes blazing with red-orange flowers. It's true that the tropical sun baked the beaches to a light golden brown, and the waters surrounding those beaches shimmered in shades of blue and green no Crayola had ever been named for. But you paid to see it. Cruisers had to post a $1,000 bond, payable in U.S. dollars and returned in French francs upon exiting French Polynesia. The idea, some said, was to limit the number of arrivals. Locals around the planet called us "water squatters" and considered us akin to seagulls, the "rats of the sea." In their view, we came into their harbors, dumped our trash, emptied our holding tanks, helped ourselves to the limited fresh water supply, and never spent enough money to make our stay worth their while. French civil servants working as harbormasters apparently shared that view.

"They're an inhospitable lot," said Marsh, after spending an unsuccessful day on paperwork that only the boat captain could complete. "I got no civilities, no English, and no entry stamp."

But if you went to church, Marsh and I discovered, the locals might forgive you your sins. We became Sunday morning regulars in island churches across the Pacific after sitting on our balcony at the Pension Gauguin in Hiva Oa on a Saturday night, listening to a choir practice for the next day's service. Their voices rose up in waves that bounced off the mountains and saturated the air around us.

"It's like surround sound," I said. "What must it be like in church?"

Like the most joyful noise unto the Lord we had ever heard, we decided the next day, as we sat in the back pew of a packed evangelical Christian church. In hymn after hymn, a strong alto voice belted out the first few notes, after which the choir seated around her joined in for the first verse. At the refrain, the rest of the congregation came in, a hundred or so mixed voices, male and female, adults and children. Fervent, confident, a cappella voices, singing in their native Marquesan, singing as if their salvation depended on it. The music rolled over the pews, up to the rafters, and through our bodies, leaving goose bumps in its wake.

After the service, we stood outside in front of the church by ourselves. Marsh wanted to go up to someone to say how much the singing had moved us. But neither of us spoke French, much less Marquesan, and we felt awkward.

A short, round woman, wearing an enormous black hat perfect for a wedding in London, approached us. She smiled, threw open her arms, and asked, "You like our church?"

"We love your church," said Marsh. "And we especially love your singing. Are you part of the choir? I can't tell you how inspiring the music was for us."

He was right about that—he couldn't tell her because she couldn't understand him. She shrugged her shoulders, smiled in apology, then pushed herself between us and put an arm around each of our waists. She pulled us toward a fig tree, which shaded other church ladies who stood behind a long, white plastic table, overloaded with platters of food: pyramids of tea sandwiches cut in triangles and squares, cake slices spread out like fans, chunks of pineapple and papaya mounded around shot glasses of toothpicks, a rainbow of cold drinks in transparent pitchers. Our new friend in the black hat shouted something to the others, who poured two drinks, piled food on plates, and beamed as they handed them to us.

The music and the welcome in Bora-Bora were even more astounding. The same exuberant cacophony of voices, but more of them, perhaps two hundred in all, sent the sound ricocheting off the ceiling ribs of the cavernous church. We listened from elevated pews to one side of the altar, where ushers had escorted the handful of foreign visitors. Leaning over and whispering in my ear, Marsh said, "The better to see you, my dear, when they pass the collection plate."

At the end of the service, ushers returned to escort the foreigners out of the church. Like border collies, they herded us down the aisle and, once outside, gently pushed and pulled us into a line beside the front door. As we stood there, feeling puzzled and not a little foolish, the members of the congregation spilled out the front door and began to file by us. One by one, the local people shook our hands and offered a greeting in whatever language they chose—French, Tahitian, English, German—some speaking softly and averting their gaze, the majority flashing smiles full of eye contact and bonhomie. Even if we didn't understand the words, we couldn't mistake the warmth of their welcome and the humility of their gesture.

Polynesian church people aside, our next stop would turn out to be Marsh's and my favorite. Rarotonga, population 9,500, the largest of the Cook Islands, and a protectorate of New Zealand, showed cruisers the famous Kiwi hospitality. For starters, the harbormaster came down to our boats to hand-deliver entry documentation. A soft-spoken, affable man, his welcome sounded genuine. This surprise, as opposed to the usual daylong drill of hunting down hidden-away offices, stern-faced officials, and enough local currency to pay for it all, enthralled Marsh. After six previous times into the breach, armed with a French or Spanish dictionary, he was disarmed by this man and paperwork in English.

"No worries about the fee," said the harbormaster. "Come find me in the next day or two, after you've had a chance to get to the bank."

To be sure, language colored our experience. Operating in English was a relief; after months in French-speaking Polynesia and Spanish-speaking Panama and the Galápagos, we could understand and be understood. Walking around town, we could chat with the locals in shops and restaurants and get a feel for life on an island in the middle of the world's largest ocean.

One afternoon we stopped to watch a lawn bowling match. Dressed in white from their caps to their sneakers, the bowlers stood out against the emerald green of the manicured grass. Most appeared to be Maoris in their fifties and sixties. Similar to bocce, lawn bowling was apparently a deliberate game of strategic moves. On taking a turn, each player walked around the green and studied it from several angles before laying down the bowl for a slow roll.

Marsh was enchanted. He approached one of the teams and asked if they would mind his joining them the next day for a round. *By all means,* they responded, delighted by his interest. Later, back on the boat, he rummaged through his clothes in search of a presentable set of whites. The next afternoon, all dressed up in them and ready to bowl, he stood on deck, where Bill spotted him. "Ah Jay-sus, will you look at this," hollered Bill, anchored two boats away. "Next thing you know, he'll be running for office."

Our stay in a local hotel took on more meaning, too, now that we could visit with the proprietors. We became friends with the Kiwi owner-manager team of Peter, a retired medical doctor, and his wife, Helen. Throughout our stay, they invited us to restaurants or over for barbecues where they hinted at an interest in additional partners to help run the hotel. It was tempting to contemplate, but in the end we deemed a plane ride to Rarotonga too arduous and expensive for us and our kids.

I was content to dawdle in Rarotonga awhile. To date we had spent equal amounts of time under sail and in port. This was not the norm—most cruisers spent far more time at anchor than under way. But Kevin and Marge were in a hurry. They only had a year of sabbatical; already it was June. They wanted to see as many dream spots as possible and hoped to join a cousin in Thailand by November. Guilt about ending the trip in Australia made me acquiesce to their desire for speed. Marsh coupled the same guilt with glee at the prospect of jumping ship altogether, so always cast his vote for leaving any port as soon as possible.

I was probably the only one with a heavy heart when we pulled anchor and waved goodbye forever to the kindliest harbormaster in the Pacific, standing on the landing dock and wishing us Godspeed. Ahead lay the archipelago of Tonga. In ten days, we would land in the Va'vau Group of the giant one hundred seventy–island kingdom. But not before enduring our most harrowing night at sea.

The end of our fifth day out of Rarotonga found us midway to our destination. After dinner, we settled into the familiar evening routine. One of us scanned the radio dial for something to listen to; two retired to their respective cabins for a read; the fourth began the first watch of the night. By 10 P.M., the wind had begun to build, and a light rain was falling. Lightning flashed off the bow and lit up the horizon. Within minutes the wind velocity increased and rain lashed into the cockpit, stinging the backs of my calves as I stood at the helm on watch. The others came up on deck in foul-weather gear, and Marsh brought along mine. We watched as the wind churned up waves—ten feet high, then fifteen feet, then twenty or more—and hurled them randomly into the cockpit to jolt whomever they drenched.

Built for the fierce North Sea storms, *St. Kilda* slid up and down the twenty-foot swells like a roller-coaster car on a well-oiled track, with soft landings in troughs before her next smooth ascent. But her jib, the only sail up, and her self-steering vane couldn't handle the gale-force winds. With a terrifying roar, the four hundred feet of canvas broke loose from the foot and exploded at the bow, where the howling wind swooped up the sail and slapped it fore and aft. Marsh and Kevin hurried into their safety harnesses, clipped themselves onto jackstays secured to the deck, and pulled themselves forward to haul in the jib. Marge shone a flashlight on them as they battled the forty-knot winds and torrents of rain for half an hour, while I turned over the engine and hung on to the wheel, trying to keep us from veering even more wildly off course.

Bad things come in threes, the saying goes, and they happened to us within minutes of each other. First, our jib blew. Second, while the men struggled at the bow, our electrical system died—no GPS now, no cockpit light to read the compass, no running lights for a tanker fifty times our size to see. And third, Marsh looked through the green water coming over the bow and spotted a sailboat off to starboard, illuminated by lightning and aimed right at us. It was stupefying—after months at sea without a single sighting of another vessel or a trace of bad weather, we were on a collision course, during a storm, at night, and without lights.

To our credit, and as luck would have it, no one got seasick or hurt, and no one panicked. Marsh and Kevin pulled in the shredded sail, we "fixed" the electricals by turning on a switch accidentally knocked off, and I hailed the other boat on the radio to tell them our course. The wind abated almost as quickly as it had come up; by midnight, all was calm and the rain had stopped. Crises averted, three of our exhausted crew went back to bed. We had passed the only weather test we would have to take on the trans-Pacific voyage.

But we made a sorry sight as *St. Kilda* limped into harbor in Va'vau, Tonga. Dirty, under bare poles, our alternator still malfunctioning, we needed to find a mechanic and a sailmaker. Va'vau had several of both, because it was a popular base camp for The Moorings, an upscale yacht chartering company. Their shiny new boats, anchored in coves off the lush little islands, made for poster-perfect photos. The snorkeling and scuba diving were spectacular: neon fish, crystalline water, underwater caverns, drop-offs thousands of feet down. The feasts staged for foreigners were fabulously hokey—we sat cross-legged on straw mats and ate with our fingers the grilled seafood and tropical fruit spread out before us on banana fronds.

But a darker side of these northern islands of Tonga was evident, even in church. Somber hymns about sin and mercy replaced the joyful noise of earlier islands. No invitation to cake and cold drinks was forthcoming this time. The crowd of big-boned, unsmiling people, the men dressed in gray wraparound skirts, the women in high-necked floral dresses, ignored us after the service. Back at the hotel, where Marsh and I had signed in for our ritual stay, we asked a clerk about the seriousness. He attributed it to the recent rapes of several young girls. Va'vau was reeling from the last one, which ended in a gruesome murder of an eight-year-old girl.

"It's because of movies," he said. "We don't have a movie theater, but VCRs have become common here in the past year or two. The sex and violence in the videos shock the men and give them horrible ideas. They are simple men who grew up in a strict religion. The modern ways they see in these videos confuse them and make them do bad things."

I can't remember exactly when Marsh declared he had had enough and needed to get off the boat for good, but Tonga might have been the place. Its depressed mood matched the one he was no longer willing to hide. Our next island group would be Fiji, with an international airport in its capital city of Suva.

"We can get off in Suva and fly to Australia. Maybe spend a few weeks driving around the east coast? Stop to see Michael and Alice?" he suggested, trying to bribe me with a visit to old Shanghai friends, back home now in Melbourne.

What could I do but agree? There was no denying the urgency in his voice, and he had been a dutiful good sport for eight months. Besides, day-tripping in a car sounded like decadent fun after the hardship of passage-making. I parlayed Marsh's suggestion of a few weeks in Australia into a few months in Australia and New Zealand, and both of us savored every day of that time as we walked up to glaciers, nestled in front of vineyard fireplaces, and drove on beaches ninety miles long.

Kevin and Marge weren't having the same good time. As Marsh had predicted, *St. Kilda* was one breakdown away from potential disaster. Somewhere between Vanuatu and Australia, a systems failure scared them enough to call it quits. After a $3,000 tow into Cairns and a consult with us, *St. Kilda* was put up for sale—neither couple could afford such big bills nor the fixes the boat required. An older English woman saw her in the Cairns marina, recognized her Lauren Giles lines, and fell in love with her. She would be reoutfitted for a life of leisure, this time harbor-hopping along the Great Barrier Reef.

Regardless of its finish, the voyage had lived up to its billing as a sail of a lifetime. And Marsh had bragging rights, after bringing us over ten thousand nautical miles from Rhode Island to Fiji. He was proud of his accomplishment and relished the admiration of his old friends and fellow sailors.

But he was tired and had aged visibly. "Jesus, Mary, and Joseph!" old friend Kathy whispered to me, on seeing him for the first time back in the U.S. "He looks like a strung-out old man. What happened to him?"

*St. Kilda* would be the last boat Marsh captained. He was sixty-five years old. After forty years on the water, his passion for sailing had been dampened, we thought, by a bad case of nerves and obsession over the many things that can and do go wrong on a boat. But this simple diagnosis was wrong. In two years we would learn the truth and the real answer to Kathy's question.

## "Remember the Sweet Things"

· for my first day of student teaching, leaving an apple on the kitchen table with "a note to the teacher."

· for hours, killing himself digging fence-post holes among the roots of hundred-year-old maple trees, placing them where I'd asked; seeing my disappointed face when I noticed that the holes were on two different planes and saying casually, "No problem. I can move them."

· MARSH, disapproving of my choice of paint color and muttering something under his breath.
ELLEN, menacingly: "What was that you said?"

MARSH, benignly: "I said I hear they fired on Fort Sumter."

• bringing me a bouquet of daffodils for no particular reason

• the pleasure of preparing for Jennifer's wedding, mainly because of his enthusiasm and willingness to pitch in on anything and everything, e.g., in his tuxedo, an hour before the ceremony, paint bucket in hand, hitting a spot we'd missed in the kitchen

• he and Jennifer fighting back tears as he walked her down the aisle at First Church in Framingham

• a great anniversary card: "American Gothic" couple + caption "Oh well, what's done is done."

• his making a quick left-hand turn in front of oncoming traffic; my scoffing and calling it a real Shanghai move; his running commentary on his next two or three turns and how "it's model driving, don't you think?"

• his always noticing when I wear something new and asking, "Is that new?" usually followed by "Looks nice. It's you."

  · the satisfaction of our getting a coat of varnish on the boat before Narragansett Bay clouded over; lunch on the afterdeck out of an Igloo cooler; spending Saturday night with Gus at Rock Rest and weathering the rum squall that passed through

  · his patience in teaching me how to start the outboard without flooding it and how to dock and secure the dinghy in a rough chop

  · hearing me scream and coming to catch a three-foot snake in the side garden; stuffing it in a canvas sack and driving it off "to a place far, far away"

  · handing me a rose by way of apology, he said, for having been "uncommunicative" the night before; truth was, he had been dog tired, and I had been going on about a topic that didn't interest him

  · packing up the house and cleaning all day; standing in the empty dining room, arms around each other, reminiscing about the weddings celebrated and dinners enjoyed in that lovely room; saying an emotional goodbye to a dear old house

  · MARSH, after a day at the boatyard working with Kevin: "I made Kevin angry."

ELLEN: "Why?"

MARSH, sheepishly: "I was hovering."

• the good omen of *St. Kilda*'s averaging an unheard-of eight knots on the first leg to Norfolk; for Commander Greene's memory's sake, saluting as we passed U.S. Navy Pier 5

• motoring down the Intracoastal Waterway, from North Carolina to Florida; taking turns driving us aground; his growing out his beard and looking salty

• my first night watch alone, going to the Bahamas; seeing a boat on fire, heading right for us, and waking him up; "That would be the moon coming up, El," he said, grinning. "But not to be embarrassed. Eternal vigilance is the price of safety at sea."

• by ourselves, the only boat anchored off Malabar Cay and a tiny, barren rock pile of an island; his waxing eloquent about "its haunting coastline, enjoyed only by the cognoscenti"

• our first long passage: fourteen days of no land in sight, going from Panama to the Galápagos; uneventful cruising but a great time onshore, taking hot showers in the funky little Hotel Angermeyer

• swimming with sea lions off Bartolomé in the Ga-lápagos

• baking cookies together in a boisterous seaway, fifteen days out and ten days away from the Marquesas

• his superb navigation, always, but especially get-ting us into Hiva Oa in the Marquesas, after twenty-five days at sea, within fifteen minutes of his estimated arrival time

• at a Sunday church service in Hiva Oa; reciting the Lord's Prayer in Marquesan

• our favorite dish at the Bora-Bora Yacht Club—poisson cru, made with fresh coconut milk; his bad-gering the reluctant French chef for the recipe until he relented and took us back into the kitchen to walk us through his instructions

• torturing us on a hot day, five days out, five more to go, with his description of a cold one: "Picture the icy cold droplets running down the side of the can. . . . Feel the cool brew sliding down your parched throat"

• the four of us sitting in the cockpit, playing Pass-word; his getting the right word, "snap," from Kevin's clues of "bean," then "shackle"; the two of them jumping up with a roar and giving each other a bear hug

• renting rusty bikes on Moorea and Huahine; circumnavigating the islands and savoring the views after tough ups to hilltops

• intermission at the movie theater in Rarotonga, i.e., turning off the projector; joining the crowd in the lobby for boysenberry ice cream cones served up by a cheerful Maori matron

• a *Cruising World* magazine moment: anchored off Va'vau in Tonga, sitting on the foredeck under the stars, sipping a 1987 Spanish rioja, listening to a church choir practicing in the distant hills

• Jennifer's surprise of joining us in Fiji

• selling *St. Kilda* in Cairns; hitting the road for a month, zigzagging down the east coast of Australia as far south as Melbourne; handing me a smoked kangaroo and brie sandwich and saying, "I know it's early, darling, but happy birthday."

• repeating the no-reservation, just-get-in-a-car-and-go experience of Australia, this time in New Zealand; his again doing all the driving so I can gawk and take photos

- our nominees for:
  - most primitive: Hiva Oa, Marquesas
  - friendliest "natives": Rarotonga, Cook Islands
  - most overrated: Tahiti, French Polynesia
  - best food: Bora-Bora Yacht Club
  - best snorkeling: Va'vau Group, Tonga
  - most picturesque island: tied, Malololailai, Fiji, and Stanley Cay, Bahamas
  - most picturesque town: Christchurch, New Zealand
  - best beaches: along the Great Ocean Road, Victoria, Australia

# Chapter 6

## *Finding a New Home:*
## *1996–1998*

MARSH AND I WERE NOW HOMELESS—NO HOUSE, no boat, no town to call our own. Finding a place to live became the de rigueur next adventure. Early on, we said we wanted no more ice and snow after Marsh retired, but that left a lot of places on the planet to consider. How about Australia? Bill had all but offered Marsh a spot in his Queensland boatbuilding business. Or New Zealand? A couple of fellow cruisers had suggested we settle near them in Whangarei on North Island. Or Mexico? Baja California and the port of La Paz was home base for a handful of American cruisers we met along the way, and they raved about it.

We reached two conclusions after round one of deliberations. First, we shouldn't stray too far away from the United States, since our kids couldn't afford the time or the ticket to come see us. Second, a new hometown had to be on a coast. Marsh had lived close to the ocean for sixty-five years. He thought he needed a break from sailing just now, but neither one of us could even conceive of his giving up boating in the long term.

"Maybe we switch to a powerboat," he said as we rested up one day in Jennifer and Patrick's San Francisco apartment, after the flight from Auckland and before heading back to Massachusetts. "We could take up deep-sea fishing. What would you think of day-tripping on a small powerboat?"

*Not much*, I thought. He had done too thorough a job of indoctrinating me on the superiority of sailboats over "stink pots." But this was not the time to squelch his enthusiasm. A tweak proved irresistible, though.

"Sure, why not?" I said. "A stuffed marlin on the wall adds so much to any room."

We came up with a house-hunting plan. A place relatively close to the kids and on a coast meant the United States, the Caribbean, or Mexico. We would pick up the Dodge Dakota truck we left in Massachusetts and drive the U.S. and Mexican coastlines, stopping in towns we heard were interesting or that caught our eye. We would load the truck with provisions for longer stays in places we might choose to explore in depth: clothes for all kinds of weather, some dishes and cookware, a few towels and bed linens, and the biggest box of books we could manage. We would consider it an open-ended trip; we would stop when it no longer felt like fun or it became too expensive. About four to six months would do it, we thought. The Caribbean we would figure out later.

Next we devised a rating system. We listed all the like-to-haves in a new place to live and weighted the factors. Three points for housing to our preference within our price range and a reasonable cost of living. Three points also for a year-round temperate climate, a teaching job opportunity for me, and an international airport nearby. Two points for a good public library, interesting sailing destinations, and top-notch eateries. One point for a university, good shopping, decent health care, and a military base nearby. Our plan was to add up the points and give the top scorer a trial run by renting there for a year.

First to be rated was Wilmington, North Carolina, last was San Francisco, California. In the six months between them, we looked at twenty-four places, including eight in Mexico. We vetted each in the same way: We found a Realtor, explained the rating system, and asked to see what the town had to offer. Good Realtors are also good tour guides—after a day or two, we usually had a decent enough feel to be able to do the math.

We learned quickly that the United States abounds in interesting coastal towns and that selecting one might be a happy problem. We loved the variety of home styles on the islands around Charleston, South Carolina. Our budget allowed for a small house on the beach in Pensacola, Florida. The Victorians of Galveston, Texas, went on for blocks, resplendent in purples and pinks. The houseboats on barges in Sausalito, California, appealed to us as a perfect transition.

We took a Christmas break and joined our kids and grandkids in Austin, Texas, the hometown of Marsh's daughters Lisa and Jen. The gag gifts we picked up along the way seemed mildly funny when we fingered them in roadside shops: seashell-infested toothpick holders, bubble gum "Cuban" cigars, Aunt Jemima salt and pepper shakers. They seemed downright hilarious when the kids unwrapped them in Austin and gave us puzzled looks that asked, "Should we be worried?"

After the holidays, we headed south for Mexico and the Spanish colonial gems of Zacatecas, Guanajuato, San Miguel de Allende, and Querétaro, to take in some historic sights as we worked our way to the Pacific. We hadn't bought a guidebook or studied up. As usual, we would be slipshod tourists, content to wander around until we became hungry or tired. But you couldn't go wrong in these stunning cities, built on high plateaus to escape the summer heat and dating back to the conquistadors. Photo opportunities appeared round every corner—cantera angels, gilded altars, talavera-tiled fountains and storefronts. It was my first time in Mexico, and the country dazzled me.

"Let's turn right and head for the coast, before you fall for one of these beauties," Marsh said.

What I had fallen for was Mexico. And the love affair continued when we reached the Pacific coast and walked along the malecón of Puerto Vallarta. The car ferry for the Baja leaves from Puerto Vallarta, a Mexican friend in Querétaro advised us. He was wrong, and later we would thank him for the mistake.

Vallarta was charming, and the charm was palpable. Locals gave us easy smiles as we strolled among them along the cobblestoned streets. Police in white shorts and pith helmets waved traffic to a stop for us and wished us a good day. Waiters waved us to come in, relax, and sample the seafood. Shy Huichol women smiled up through their eyelashes as we examined their wares.

We checked into a hotel on the beach, with rooms for $25 a night and balconies just big enough for two white plastic chairs. "To Vallarta," Marsh said as we clinked our Coronas and watched the sun set over the Bay of Banderas, "where the beers are as cold as tits on a frog and the sky as blue as a Dutchman's pants."

The next morning we went looking for a Realtor. Sam, a Canadian who had lived in Vallarta for twelve years, trooped us through a few condos in the hills overlooking the city and a funky "house of tile" in Gringo Gulch, an old part of town popular with foreigners.

"Go north ten or twenty miles," Sam said. "Check out the little towns and villages lining the bay and up the Pacific coast before making a decision about Vallarta. I don't know the market, but I hear it's cooking up."

We took his advice. We walked the beaches of a handful of fishing villages and zigzagged through the towns for a cursory look. Then it was on to Mazatlán, the actual ferry landing on the mainland, where we crossed the Sea of Cortez to Baja California and followed the Baja coast from La Paz down to San José del Cabo, across to Mulege, and up to Ensenada. The Spanish I learned in Costa Rica and Marsh learned in Spain came back to us as we went along; we felt comfortable and welcome everywhere.

"Señor, you speak Spanish VERY well," the young waiters and hotel clerks would say to Marsh, who in truth was more self-confident than fluent. The Mexicans were being kind with him, as they were with anyone who made an effort in Spanish, even as they poked a little fun. "Grathias, MUY amable," he would play along, affecting the lisp not heard outside of Spain in the baritone of a thespian playing to the balcony. He usually got a laugh.

We crossed back into the United States and took a break from hometown-hunting. We had raved about Australia's park system without knowing much of anything about our own. So we made a swing now through some of America's best—Painted Desert, Mesa Verde, Arches, the Great Sand Dunes, the Grand Canyon. Their names alone should have tipped us off as to how spectacular they would be. The Frugal Yankee seemed especially taken with the "Golden Age Passport" that got us into some of the parks. He now carried it in his wallet and loved to flash it, cute as a grandpa showing photos of the babies. "Look—for only ten bucks. Any federal park, free, for the rest of my life," he would rave.

Our travel routine remained the same. Coffee in the motel room first thing, about seven o'clock, from the coffeemaker we brought along with us, a news show on television as we showered and packed up. Refills for the roadie cups around ten o'clock, at a Dunkin' Donuts if we were lucky enough to find one. Breakfast and lunch from a cooler, in order to steer clear of fast-food places and fried temptation. The cooler restocked at grocery stores along the way with cheese, sausage, fruit, crudités, and milk, to go with the backpack of crackers, rolls, cookies, and cereal. National Public Radio whenever and for as long as possible, then switching music stations the rest of the way—classical for him, country and western for me; singing out loud when we remembered the words. Changing drivers every three or four hours. Lots of comfortable silence, thinking our own thoughts—neither of us could read in the car without getting a headache. Frequent pats on the leg or strokes of the arm, apropos of nothing. Stopping for the night around sunset and watching *The News Hour* on PBS before dinner out, at the nicest place a motel clerk could recommend.

But as we returned to the hunt and worked our way up the West Coast, from San Diego to San Luis Obispo to San Francisco, we seemed to lose interest. We stopped seeking out Realtors. After spending a few hours driving down a few main streets, we declared this California town to be identical to the one we had just passed through. Back in Jennifer and Patrick's apartment in San Francisco, we convinced ourselves it was a waste of time to go on—we wouldn't be happy in the gray and rain of the Northwest. We had seen enough. The odyssey was over.

We had our three top contenders, all in the U.S. The bronze went to Beaufort, South Carolina, with its classy new marina and waterfront. It combined small-town friendly with big-city convenient, sitting so close to Charleston and Atlanta. San Diego, California, took the silver: best weather in the country, world-class beach and zoo, a perfect base camp for getaways up and down the U.S. and Mexican coasts. And, after six months on the road crossing countless state lines, we awarded the gold to Savannah, Georgia. Savannah of the twenty-four town squares, affordable historic homes, and one-day sail to the Bahamas.

We made our decision. We decided to ignore the scores and the winners. Instead we picked a tiny town in Mexico that hadn't even made it into the Top Ten.

Bucerias, Nayarit, population 6,000, got the nod as our new hometown. On the Bay of Banderas and ten miles north of Puerto Vallarta, the red brick arches of its homes and the brilliant rosa Mexicana bougainvilleas spilling over garden walls hit a nerve. We hadn't thought to rate raw natural beauty during our search for a new hometown. Yet it now turned out to be the determining factor. Never mind that most of the small shops could have used a coat of paint, or that no public works department existed to pick up trash, or that water bubbled up from leaking lines and poured down some of the streets. The long, white sand walking beach and the sound of the gentle surf made us overlook all that. We renamed the scruffiness "local color."

It helped that the bay area had begun to boom at about the time of our arrival. We sat on the small balcony of a rented apartment, feet up on the rail, glasses of wine in hand, as we watched the sun set and listened to other gringos walking below, looking at empty lots for sale on either side of our building.

"This one looks good."

"Jot down that number."

"If we drag our feet, we'll lose out again," we heard them saying, sunset after sunset.

After a few weeks of eavesdropping, we started to feel anxious. "Maybe we should get in on this, before it's too late," Marsh said.

Why not? we figured. In what seemed like a hot real estate market, how could we lose? If a fishing town in Mexico lost its allure and we changed our minds, we could sell and move on. So we abandoned the plan of a trial run and went looking for a Realtor again. Show us some houses, we said.

Every place appealed to us. We gushed about the banana trees in the front yard of one and swooned over a mango tree in the backyard of another. A third included a swimming pool the size of a truck tire.

"Oh my God, we could have a pool," I said.

But all the homes seemed overpriced—more expensive than in the American South and without amenities like garages, storage space, and nice appliances. Okay for vacationers but not for full-timers like us. We had already decided on only one home. More than one would tie us down and make for too much concentration on "stuff"; buying, maintaining, and worrying about two households full of possessions didn't appeal. Better to hit the road during the hot summer and spend three months or so visiting the kids and seeing more of the world.

Let's build, we said, after a week of looking. Neither of us had built a house before, but how hard could it be?

We had lived in a lot of different houses and knew what we liked and didn't like about them. We could make lists of those things and discuss them with an architect. In Spanish, even.

We got right on it. First we traversed the town, looking for the office of a builder and asking for names in hardware stores. That's how we found Frank, a German engineer married to a Mexican teacher he met in Munich. Frank had been building in Bucerias for the past six years and was happy to show us some of the projects he had completed, along with his Mexican architect-partner, Jorge.

We bounced Frank's name off the gringos we often met at Café Magana, a ribs restaurant we all frequented, and he received good reviews. All attested to his engineering skills, fair pricing, and adherence to a budget. Plus Geoff, ex-footballer from Manchester, England, and owner of Café Magana, was probably right when he said, "A German engineer and a Mexican designer? I call that a dream team."

That was good enough for us; Frank would be our guy.

"You will receive no surprises from me," Frank said. "We agree on thirty-four dollars per square foot, and that is what you will pay." He turned out to be true to his word and to our contract.

Finding a piece of land proved just as easy. Again,

we got lucky wandering around town, asking questions. This time we found Apolonio. Standing at his front gate and overhearing us speculate about the empty lot next door, he stepped forward and introduced himself as a pest-control specialist–cum–real-estate broker. He assured us that he could convince the owner of this lot to sell for a commission of, say, 8 percent. He was a recently converted Jehovah's Witness, he said, and honest beyond reproach. His appearance, however, conveyed a different message—short and squat with slicked-back hair and a handlebar mustache, he bore an unfortunate resemblance to the Frito Bandito sans sombrero.

But Apolonio delivered as promised. Within days, and accompanied by Frank, we were sitting in the landowner's Puerto Vallarta office, signing papers, while Apolonio paced outside the window. He had earned his 8 percent, we commented to the Mexican owner, an apparently successful businessman who spoke of several other properties he had for sale.

"Eight percent? That would be generous to the point of ridiculous," said the owner. "I know him. He lives by his wits and will take what he can get. Give him two percent."

We gave him 4 percent. It was a gorgeous piece of land, after all, at an excellent price. The property ran the length of a city block, down a hill scattered with mango, papaya, and banana trees. A white stucco one-bedroom bungalow sat midway and off to one side; it needed work but had good sturdy lines and a fine aged-tile roof. Six-foot-high red brick walls, still in good condition, enclosed the sixteen-thousand-square foot property from top to bottom. When the building crew began cleaning up, they uncovered still more red brick and masonry. For fifteen years, the land had lain untouched, and eroded soil had buried two patios and a winding pathway that connected them, plus a cobblestoned parking lot inside the lower gate. And, best part of all, our newly acquired land had an uninterrupted view that swept across the bay. The vistas ensured us a sensational home.

Marsh and I went to work listing our ideas for a small, one-story house, not sure we could afford all of them but listing them anyway:

· one large room to serve as kitchen and dining and living room

· a master bedroom and bath at one end of the house

· two small bedrooms with a shared bath at the other end

· a study, as a dehumidified space for electronics and books

· a deep, wide porch across the front, facing a swimming pool

Jorge took it from there and made drawings, by hand, which Frank costed out.

"We can do it," he declared. "I can build everything on your wish list, within your budget, and even throw in a viewing area on the roof." We were beside ourselves.

Armed with camera and sketchpad, we scoured the streets of Bucerias and Puerto Vallarta, looking for ideas for windows and doors, grillwork, and landscaping. A Vallarta charity ran house tours as a fund-raiser, and we became regulars, intent on stealing ideas for our interior. We pretended to be potential buyers of homes featured in glossy magazines and walked through a lot of them, too, with the same intention. I bought, borrowed, and pored over countless coffee-table books with titles like *Casas de la Costa*. We took the ideas to evening meetings with Jorge and Frank, who incorporated many of them into the design.

Two months after arriving in Bucerias "to give it a try," we broke ground on the house we would name "Quinta Elena," after the lady of the house and according to Mexican tradition.

The bungalow already on the property proved to be a godsend, albeit a termite-ridden haven for cockroaches and wolf spiders when we first looked inside. We would live in it while the main house was under construction. We gave Frank some ideas for fixing it up, then took off for a few months of visits in the States with our kids.

For a few thousand dollars, his crew transformed it into a comfortable little talavera-tiled jewel, complete with a new covered porch big enough for a table, four chairs, and a barbecue.

Frank had another good idea, too—to build the swimming pool while we were gone and have it ready for our return. Going for a swim after the crew left turned out to be the relaxation we needed, after days of scavenger hunting in Vallarta or waiting for no-show subcontractors at the site.

Conventional wisdom said to stay put during construction—no detail was too small not to be overseen by the owner. So, on our return, we did just that for the next ten months. But our motivation had more to do with our own enjoyment than fear of mistakes. We were getting a custom-built house because there was no alternative. It was the only way most crews knew how to build. In our case, the crew followed only two pages of blueprints, which left scores of engineering and design decisions to be made every day, live and on-site. "Just-in-time" construction, we called it. Other gringos called it "by-the-seat-of-your-pants" and preferred to bring detailed architectural drawings from home.

No prints existed for an arch under our kitchen counter, for instance, or for an "ojo de buey" window over the front door, or for a cupola that would rise above the dining room table. We and Goyo, the chief mason, talked each one of them through, sometimes brick by brick. It was a first-time creative process for us, and we enjoyed ourselves.

At Café Magana in the evening, we heard fellow homebuilders repeat more than enough times, "If the marriage can survive building a house, it can survive anything." For us, it wasn't such a strain. We had issues with Frank and Jorge that resulted in hand-wringing and shouts, to be sure. But not with each other. For starters, we agreed on how much we would spend and we kept to that number. Honoring the budget was more important to Marsh than to me; I knew we could afford some slippage. I also knew it would have made him anxious and therefore taken away some of the satisfaction this project was giving him. So when the masons laid the first room with the floor tile slated for the rest of the house, too, and I saw how much I disliked what I had chosen, I let it lie. To take up the tile, return it, and buy something else would have meant a budget overrun. I also settled for substandard appliances when we neared the end of construction and money was tight. In the long run, this was a mistake, but I made it to appease my partner.

For his part, Marsh gave me my head when it came to aesthetics. This was easy for him to do, in the sense that I cared much more than he did about where to place wall niches or how wide to make the windows or which plumbing fixtures to use. But it was kind of him, too, in that he knew that I didn't know as much as I sometimes pretended. His questioning my judgment would have shaken my confidence and taken away some of the fun that I was having. Not only did he not question my judgment, he was quick to praise my choices, in private and in public. Whenever someone complimented us on the house, he stretched the truth and told them, "Ellen gets all the credit. Almost everything in here was her idea."

Our speaking Spanish played a big part in our enjoyment of the building process, too. We reached a level of comfort with the crew and made decisions together easily.

"Marshall, how many steps should I make down to the pool house?" Alberto, another of the masons, asked one day.

"I don't know. Maybe eight?" answered Marsh.

Alberto paused for a minute, contemplated the bare patch of dirt before him, and said, "I think seven would be enough."

"Well, you know best," said Marsh.

Alberto grabbed handfuls of lime from a bag nearby and dropped lines of white dust in the dirt. He would follow this "print" when he built the seven steps.

"Alta tecnología," said Marsh, and both of them chuckled.

Either you liked this casual, undocumented approach

or it scared you and made you go ugly early over "these people" and "whatever could they have been thinking." We liked it. Maybe it was because we had no big cock-ups or redos over the course of the construction. Or maybe it was because we set the bar low and were content to live with the little mistakes. Like the incredible hulk of a candelabra we couldn't refuse, when delivered by an ironworker and friend, beaming with pride. Or the miscalculated gift of "Quinta Elena" spelled out in black sea stones and set in cement, but without enough space for the final *a*. "The grace of imperfection," we called it.

Plenty of gringos built beautiful houses without saying a word to their crew because they either spoke no Spanish or were absentee owners who worked with English-speaking architects and builders. It was doable, but also their loss. The masons had clever ideas they didn't always share with the architect, given the hierarchical Mexican world of work. But they loved to point out to us the architect's oversights or to present us with creative additions not included in the print. That's how we came to have "eyebrows" (little roofs) over each of our windows, which kept out the rain during the torrential summer storms, and decorative "Aztec suns" at the top of our porch columns, made from hand-rounded pieces of red brick.

"It is a pleasure for us, too, Señora Elena, when we

can talk to the owners," said Martin, our foreman and head of the local masons' union. As an older married woman and a teacher, I always merited an honorific of "Señora" or "Doña" and the more formal "usted" versus an informal "tu."

"When you speak to us in Spanish, we can better give you what you want. It is frustrating when the owners can't make us understand. If only I spoke more English, I could make that easier." He had bought so many books and paid for so many English lessons over the years, he said, but he was a "bruto," and the words didn't stick.

I had heard Mexicans lament their inability to communicate with foreign "guests" before, as if they were ill-mannered hosts. I gave silent thanks to my old Spanish professor at Madison who made me hold a lit candle before my mouth, practicing *p*'s and *t*'s until I could say them with no trace of a flicker. Not that I didn't make glaring mistakes regularly, but I sounded pretty when I did. This had the effect of raising the comfort level of the listener, who would become more expansive when chatting with me, perhaps considering me more fluent than I actually was.

I talked a lot with Martin, sometimes in English so he could try to move beyond beginner's level, but mostly in Spanish. He liked to give me lessons in his version of Mexican history and current events. An ardent socialist, he seethed at the ejiditarios (holders of government land grants) going to bed with developers and selling off communal lands.

"Soon we'll be right back where we were before the last revolution, with millions of peasants landless again, because they didn't have the foresight to hang on to their birthright," he said. "Selling for a few miserable dollars what will turn into fortunes for the rich foreigners and Mexicans who appeal to their need and their greed," Martin said, taking a paternalistic view of his country-men. Others disagreed. Didn't the poor have the same right as anyone else to get in on the current coastal land rush?

Immigration was another favorite topic. He and most of the others on the crew had done a stint "alla" (over there, meaning the U.S.) as illegals and were happy to find full-time work at home.

"It's true that an apprentice mason can make more in Fresno in the fields than here," Martin admitted. "But wages here on the coast are going up, your family is covered by the national health care plan, and you are building a future and a pension. Your country and your family need you here."

It sounded like a stump speech he might have deliv-ered during his run for union president. He lightened up and went on.

"Anyway, I'd rather ride my bike to work under a warm sun and go home to sleep with my wife. Over there, I drove an old beater that wasn't worth the trouble it caused me or the gas I put in it. For two years, I lived with eight other guys in a filthy apartment we were too tired to clean and too broke to heat. Ay no. Never again."

Like most people living in a foreign country, Marsh and I savored the cross-cultural education we received from the locals. Among the many lessons we learned from our building crew, one of the most endearing was how to milk a situation for every last drop of a good time. Take, for instance, our deciding on paint colors with Marcos, the painting contractor. As he hand-mixed the colors and applied big squares on the porch as samples, masons sauntered by, as if by chance, and stopped to offer their opinions. The porch wall filled with the cobalt blues, egg yolk yellows, and hot pinks I was asking for, and the crew chimed right in, apparently as enthusiastic about the vibrant colors as I.

"More heat in the pink, Marcos. That pink looks like a big wad of bubble gum," one of them said.

"That yellow will be orange in the late-afternoon sun. It could be pretty, though," said another.

"I like the blue, Señora. It's beautiful," another one said. "Maybe you could put it on two walls in the dining room instead of one."

"It's better on just one wall," one of the young apprentice masons said. "It'll stand out more."

"Ay carajo," the rest hooted, with Martin chiming in, "What a waste—an artist, hauling buckets of cement!"

Or take the crew's reaction to our son-in-law, Patrick, when he and Jennifer joined us for the Christmas holidays. I came up the stairs from the bungalow to find him next to the pool, slathering suntan lotion on his six foot four inches of pale Irish skin. I looked up and saw eight men, standing on the roof in a straight line, arms folded across their chests, staring silently at Pat.

"What?" I asked them, raising my arms and flicking my wrists.

"It's your son-in-law, Señora. We have never seen a man so white," said Martin. "Blanco, blanco, blanco. Casi transparente."

Pat didn't need a translation, and laughed along with everyone else.

"You should take a photo," said Goyo. "We'll send down our darkest guy."

Down came Abel, the youngest crew member, if not the darkest. He stood next to Pat and reached up to put an arm around his shoulder, while co-workers hooted derisions and I took pictures.

"Abel, is it true that you're the black sheep of the family?"

"Make like an eclipse, Abel, and stand in front of Patricio."

The group of us had another good laugh at our "tag

sale." Our United Van Lines shipment arrived earlier than expected, after a boat ride from Boston and an overland drive from Veracruz. We made our final sort back in Westborough before jumping aboard *St. Kilda,* and we didn't have the tropics in mind. Six pairs of skis came off the truck, along with a bag of turtleneck sweaters, a box of Hudson Bay wool blankets, and two red snow shovels.

Also in the shipment were "good" dishes and "every-day" dishes, "good" flatware in silver and "everyday" flat-ware in stainless steel. We unwrapped what now seemed like a ridiculous accumulation of bowls, platters, pots and pans, bed linens, table linens, and towels. Having this number of duplicates embarrassed us at this stage in our lives and in this part of the world, where so many had so little. We set aside the monogrammed silver "G-ware" for Lisa, Marsh's oldest, then arranged duplicates and unneeded items on planks running the length of the porch, prepared to offer them all to the men.

But how would we do that without insulting them? I worried that we would send an unintended demean-ing message: "Here, this stuff isn't good enough for us anymore, so you can have it."

Marsh was more pragmatic. An hour before quitting time, he took Martin to the porch, walked him down the planks for a look at the giveaways, and said, "Look, we have lots more than we need here. Can you and the guys help us out by taking some of it off our hands?"

"Not a problem," said Martin. He put two fingers between his teeth and whistled for the others.

As they gathered around, Martin repeated Marsh's request. Some of the crew nodded, straight-faced and solemn; others smiled and headed straight for the goods. No one seemed insulted. In short order, they were kidding about whose wife would look good in which sweater, and pretending to argue over who would take home a monstrous lobster platter bigger than most of their kitchen tables.

"Do you have a mirror handy, Señora Elena?" asked Alberto. "I'd like to see how great I look in this hat." He did look great, too, and Marsh's Calgary Stampede cowboy hat had its new owner.

Everything went, including the skis. Goyo thought they would be colorful in his garden, propping up banana trees when they bore fruit. It took us the rest of the week to haul everyone's selections to their homes, where we were met with much fanfare and given more credit than was our due.

The pouring of the concrete roof marks the official finale of building a house in Mexico, and we celebrated it with the traditional roasted chickens and cases of beer for the crew. It was bittersweet for us. We would miss these guys, after ten months together and lots of laughs. We toasted them with shots of Cazadores, our favorite tequila. Marsh spoke for both of us when he held his glass high and said, "You are more than masons, you are artisans. You have filled this home with beauty and goodwill, and our family thanks all of you . . ." He petered out, too choked up to continue. The crew loved it. They applauded and whistled, then raised their glasses to him in return.

## "Remember the Sweet Things"

· looking for lodging at the Navy base in Jacksonville; his returning the salute from a young MP at the gate and loving it; his being so pleased with the buzz cut he got for $3 at the PX

· relaxing on a deck overlooking South Carolina marshland and his commenting, "A refulgent view, wouldn't you say?"

· in a motel room in Biloxi, Mississippi, watching a movie; his reaching for my hand and saying, "I love you and our rich life."

· my scoffing at a seventysomething gyrating wildly out on the dance floor in Cabo San Lucas with a woman half his age; Marsh smiling and saying, "The lion still rules the barranca."

· sitting down and moving close to him on a sofa; his smiling and saying, "Go away. Don't sit so close to me. I hate it."

· driving alongside Lake Pontchartrain, past a statue of the Blessed Virgin; his shouting out the window, "Hail, Mary!"

· opening the last peanut or spreading the last cracker or dipping the last chip, and always offering it to me

· giving each other a high five whenever we cross a state line

· when stuck with twin beds, a quick cuddle in one or the other, last thing at night and first thing in the morning

· the ritual of reading to each other from the *New York Times*: one of us chuckles, the other smiles and says, "What?" The chuckler shares the amusing item or clever turn of phrase

• his opening the car windows while driving through Chattanooga and belting out chorus and verse of "Chattanooga Choo-choo"

• lucking out at Fort Huachuca and scoring Distinguished Visitor's Quarters; taking photos of us playing house and staying until they kicked us out

• my complimenting him on how entertaining he is as a travel companion; his wriggling and grinning, saying, "Yeah, I am, aren't I."

• telling me he looks forward to unpacking our shipment and rereading the Sweet Things lists he's stored away

• a temperature of 70 degrees at the hacienda inn in Alamos, Sonora; his lighting a fire in our room anyway, "for the romance of it"

• on our tiny balcony in Bucerias for sunset; watching the bats swoop down from the roof; chuckling at the passing pickups, loaded down with people who are lost in clouds of exhaust smoke

• walking down to the Bucerias fish market and tortilleria together, shopping for dinner makings

• he who detests shopping, traversing Puerto Vallarta with me, searching for that recommended backstreet tile store or that upstairs bamboo curtain maker, etc.

• ELLEN: "Do these pants make me look fat?"
MARSH, emphatically: "No!"
ELLEN: "Would you tell me if they did?"
MARSH, emphatically: "Yes!" Pauses, then
     mutters, "Now there's a couple of no-brainers."

• his bending low to watch a firefly lighting up a hole in the step; looking up with delight written all over his face

• our ritual after the construction crew (and their radio!) left for the day: a swim + a glass of wine on the pool house roof, watching the sunset

• waving to "my tire man" whenever he passes the roadside llanteria shack

• being so pleased with his new grass ("my best ever") and cactus garden

- his taking care of the scary stuff: fishing an iguana out of the pool, squashing big brown spiders, catching mice in the kitchen and rats in the bodega

- our good cop/bad cop routines with the builder, as we push for windows and doors before the rainy season begins

- our three-mile beach walks from Bucerias to Nuevo Vallarta; stopping for a cold beer under a palapa before heading back

- being the new expats on the block and feeling swamped with invitations; our strategizing on how to refuse some of them without seeming like snobs

- his great idea of giving each of the masons a top-of-the-line trowel as a Christmas gift

- a pomegranate sitting on the newly tiled kitchen counter, on top of a note reading,

A La Señora Ellen Greene,

Te amo.

Atentamente,

Marshall Whitney Greene

• the crew's enjoying his joining them for a few beers after work on Saturdays

• our loving attention to detail while building Quinta Elena and our intense pride in the finished product

# Chapter 7

## *At Quinta Elena:*
## *1999–2003*

THE COCONUT PALMS LEANING OVER THREE MILES of walking beach, the masses of blossoms climbing up and over stone walls, the competing light shows of sunrise and sunset saturating the sky—what struck a nerve with us also dazzled our family and friends. Bucerias, Nayarit, was a hit, and our bedrooms were occupied with guests for the high season of November to May.

Tropical Mexico overloaded our senses as we adjusted to new sounds, sights, and smells. Roosters hadn't gotten the word about sunrise and crowed all day. Chacalaca birds screeched from their perches in the "gringo trees," nicknamed for their bark that reddened and peeled. Tree lizards whistled to each other, like dog owners calling for their pets. Crickets chirped; waves pounded; palm fronds swished in the ocean breeze. The cacophony of noise morphed into a lullaby as we and our guests nodded over our paperbacks and napped in the hammock on the porch.

Not everyone felt the same. "I can't go to sleep, Grammy—there's too much to look at," said our two-year-old granddaughter, staring out the window above her bed.

The sights in our garden alone could entertain her for hours. Hummingbirds, bees the size of jawbreakers, and swarms of yellow butterflies gorged themselves on lavender Leticia blossoms and tangerine llamarada clusters that clung to the walls of the compound. Bougainvilleas in vibrant pinks, oranges, magentas, and whites, on trees ten feet tall, ran up and down the edges of the property, their thorny branches discouraging intruders. Within months of planting, flowers with colors as vivid as their names bloomed along walkways and filled terrace gardens: golden yellow "cups of gold," shiny red "bishop's balls," deep purple "mother-in-law's tongue," neon pink and orange "moments of love."

The house and bungalow overlooked a flourishing orchard. Banana, guayaba, lime, papaya and mango trees, already mature when we arrived, produced more fruit than we could eat and sent sweet smells wafting up to the porch. Six coconut palms graced the grounds. A cocotero named Mario cleaned them twice a year, when guests were around to watch the show. Barefoot, a rope around his waist and a machete in hand, he shinnied to the top of each fifty-foot tree, where he whacked off drooping fronds, cleaned out spider nests, and lowered bunches of coconuts he would later sell on the beach for their milk.

Marsh planted a cactus garden inside the orchard. It featured a century cactus that began as a six-inch gift from a friend and grew into a photo opportunity, towering over guests posed in front of it. I planted an herb garden. It thrived outside the kitchen door. Rosemary, mint, basil, oregano, and thyme crowded the small space and fired their fragrances at us through the kitchen window we always kept open.

We felt as proud of Quinta Elena as we had of 29 West. We loved being hosts and never tired of the drill with arriving guests. Marsh would put on his "airport hat" and head for Puerto Vallarta to meet planes that usually landed midafternoon; I would stay home and arrange drinks and hors d'oeuvres for sunset on the viewing deck. Within minutes of piling into the house, our friends and family would change into shorts, come out to the pool, take in their first long facefuls of tropical sun, and accept with two eager hands the margarita Marsh had ready for them.

Legendary margaritas, by the way. Everyone left Bucerias with a Mexican lime squeezer and Marsh's easy-to-remember recipe of one-one-one-and-two: one part freshly squeezed lime juice, one part freshly squeezed orange juice, one part Controy (a Mexican Cointreau knockoff), and two parts tequila. Nobody forgot their headache the next day, either, if they ignored the bartender's warning and drank more than two.

We entertained a lot at Quinta Elena. Expats were moving into the bay area in droves, many of them baby boomers investing in second homes or changing their lifestyles. And looking for new friends. We liked nothing better than inviting people to our house for dinner, and spent hours together in the kitchen, preparing elaborate meals for Priscilla and Mike, a psychoanalyst and a school psychologist from Denver; Mary and Ed, a marketing manager and a computer programmer from Berkeley; and Linda and Isaac, television producers from New York.

It was fun to fuss. And easy, with supermarkets and gourmet food shops half an hour away in Vallarta. Marsh's specialty was soup; he especially liked to make gazpacho and Basque garlic soup. I liked to use local seafood and make my favorites—coconut shrimp, red snapper in a citrus sauce, and mahi-mahi with a hazelnut tapenade. We brought out the Shanghai steamers for Mongolian hot pot, our signature dish in Bucerias. We filled the steamers with chicken broth, placed burners beneath them, and arranged three people before each "hot pot," along with plates of shrimp, chicken, fish, spinach, and bok choy. Using our best bamboo chopsticks, each trio dropped the bites of raw food into the hot broth to cook and tried hard to retrieve them without resorting to forks. We rewarded their efforts with a finish of spoons, bowls, and bean-curd threads thrown into the now enriched broth, for a dessert of noodle soup.

A lovely home. New friends. Health and happiness. Life was good. All we needed to make it complete was a dog.

At least according to Michael, who had come for a visit, found a job, and stayed. He rented our bungalow the first year and huddled over his computer from midnight to morning, taking advantage of cheaper long-distance rates while he launched an Internet marketing business. Now living in Vallarta, he called Marsh with an offer.

"There's this puppy," he began, before Marsh cut him off.

"No, Michael. No, no, and no," he said. "You've got the wrong pig by the ear if you think I'm making a fifteen-year commitment to a dog at my age." He spoke from experience. He had a dog sleeping next to his bed since childhood; only China and the boat trip had stopped us from having a pet.

Michael persisted. The puppy was a two-month-old yellow Labrador, the runt of the litter, and the cutest thing he'd ever seen. She was given to a friend as a gift.

But the friend's older female poodle didn't take to her and picked fights with the little Lab. The puppy would have to go. And what could be a more perfect new home than Quinta Elena?

I sided with Marsh. We traveled out of Mexico or within it for weeks at a time. Arranging for dog sitters would be too much of a hassle, much less the hassle of training a puppy.

Michael backed off and hung up, but bagged us the next morning when Marsh sat down at the computer. The desktop had been changed. On-screen, a yellow Lab puppy, resting in the palm of a familiar hand, stared back at Marsh, and an e-mail message read, "Please, Daddy, can we keep her?"

I caved the minute I laid eyes on the photo. When retelling the story over the years, Marsh always insisted that he had stayed strong. He called Michael and said, "I'll just take a look at her. No promises, though."

As if a soft touch like him had a chance when the honey-colored two-month-old sashayed over to him and sniffed his boat shoe. He picked her up and held her trembling body against his chest as I drove us to her new home.

We named her Lola. Soon people in Bucerias talked about "Marsh and Lola" as much as "Marsh and Ellen." They were regulars at the beach every morning, and Lola joined the other dogs in chasing each other along the water's edge, then crashing into the surf after sticks and Frisbees. On their way home, they always stopped to visit Cal at his art studio and to chat with Dean, out walking his dog Bonita. When Marsh ran errands in the car, Lola rode shotgun. Some days were too hot to leave her alone in the car, but he hated to disappoint her. So he hid the car keys in his pocket and slipped out the front door when she wasn't looking.

The three of us were crazy about Lola. Nobody had the heart to get serious about training, she was so gentle and friendly. Other than chewing a carpet corner or two as a puppy, she stayed out of trouble and trained herself on some of the basics: to poop and pee outside; to keep her nose out of people food; to wait patiently for Marsh to wake up in the morning, resting her chin on his side of the bed and eyeing him silently. But we let her get away with a lot. She drank out of toilets, goosed people as they came in the front gate, and heeled when it suited her.

Marsh took a fair amount of kidding from the other dog-walking regulars, in particular a snowbird named Otto. According to Marsh, he could count on Otto for the same greeting every October when they first met on the street, headed for the beach with their pets.

"Nice to see you again, Marsh. And I see your dog is as well trained as ever," he would say, his Doberman heeling smartly at his side, while Lola strained against the leash, gasping for air as she hauled Marsh toward the surf.

However, we did take seriously a warning about puppies drowning in swimming pools. "It happens all the time around here," said Wensislaus, our veterinarian. "Help Lola help herself. Throw her in your pool and let her practice finding her own way to the steps. Two or three minutes ought to do it."

We complied, and Michael, Marsh, and I suited up for the Big Event. Like overanxious parents, we stood around the pool, fluffy towels at the ready for a victory rubdown, while Marsh held Lola and gave her a pep talk.

"You'll be fine, Lola. And we'll be right here if you need us. See the steps over there in the corner? Just head for the steps, little girl."

But he couldn't bring himself to throw her in. He handed her to Michael, who lobbed the puppy underhand into the middle of the pool. She popped her head out of the water, a panic-stricken look in her eyes, and made for the side. Unable to scale it, she turned and headed back for the center, while we yelled at her to head for the steps, Lola, head for the stairs.

She paddled in tight little circles in the middle of the pool, creating a whirlpool that trapped her in place. We couldn't stand it. Twenty seconds into the exercise, three panicky adults leaped into the pool and grabbed for Lola, probably putting her in the most danger of drowning she faced that day. Michael reached her first. He yanked her out of the water, then carried her to a towel warming in the sun and tried to wrap her in it. Lola refused and squirmed free. She gave herself a good shake, shot Michael a reproachful look, and flounced off in a huff.

Her next time in, accompanied by a "lifeguard," Lola showed off by paddling around the perimeter, head held high, before climbing the steps out of the pool. We beamed and raved about her bravery, as if bloodlines had nothing to do with the behavior of this Labrador retriever.

Marsh was a good retiree, content with taking Lola for walks on the beach and filling his life with leisure. He bought a share in a panga, the local powerboat of choice, and took up fishing. He played tennis every week with Pancho the metalworker, "Profe" the grade-school principal, and Luis the real estate broker. He spent hours in his shop working with wood, making picture frames and refinishing furniture. Every Friday he cooked enough rice to fill a turkey roaster, filled jugs with one hundred gallons of purified water from our system, and drove to a "feed-the-children" site to help dish out a free meal.

Fifteen years younger, with zero interest in sports, I needed more to do, and Mexican public schools had a constant need for teachers of English as a Second Language. So I signed on with CETMAR, a federal vocational high school in La Cruz, the next town over, where I taught four classes of juniors and seniors.

These teenagers were charmers who would have delighted any teacher. They were normal kids—dogs ate their homework; mystery viruses attacked them when the surf was up. But their self-regulating in the classroom would have amazed my U.S. counterparts. I needed only one disciplinary trick to keep order: If I stopped talking to them, they stopped talking to each other. And looked sheepish.

Forty students to a group, each group took all its classes together for the three years of high school, so the members grew close to each other. Close enough to hiss and boo when two boys crossed a line in a skit and threw "fuckin' awesome" into their dialogue. Or to howl their disapproval of a sassy young woman who knew better than to speak to me in Spanish with the overly familiar "tu" form of "you."

Custom dictated lovely manners. If I tried to clean the board, someone always ran up to take the eraser from my hand, smile, and ask, "¿Me permite, Maestra?" If I walked across the campus, juggling an unwieldy stack of papers or lugging a cassette player, a student invariably stepped up to help. If a group was on break and having a snack when I entered the room, no one felt comfortable eating in front of me until someone offered me a chip or a cucumber stick.

Custom also dictated that no student enter a room without asking permission of the teacher. That meant forty kids took turns at the door, asking, "May I come in, please?" They needed permission to leave the room, too, which made my policy on trips to the bathroom a counter-cultural joke. I put a felt-tip pen on my desk, with instructions to take it, no explanation required, and return promptly so the next one could go. You know, one kid at a time out of the room, without disrupting the flow of the class? It didn't work. Time and again, a student came up for the pen, turned to the others with a shrug, received an encouraging "Eso!" from classmates, then stood at the door on return to say, "May I come in, please?" I retired the pen.

By U.S. standards, theirs was a bare-bones third-world education. There were no art classes or music programs. No language labs or computer centers with Internet access. No lockers or showers; no gym for sports or dances. No books—the teachers ran off copies, and the kids paid for them. They paid for their tests, too. Fifty centavos a sheet.

But I like to think they received other things from their public school that hefty property taxes can't buy. These kids belonged. They belonged to a tight group of forty others, to begin with. The affection they felt for each other was demonstrable; the help they gave each other on assignments impressive. No one was ostracized; loners self-selected to remain aloof. In my three years at CETMAR, I never witnessed a deliberate unkind act in my classroom—these kids bore with or laughed off the loudmouth, the mentally challenged, the too-cool-for-school, the deaf-mute, the prima donna with the only cell phone who asked to be excused every twenty minutes "to take a very important call."

They belonged to a community, too. As their mission, the CETMAR high schools, all thirty-two of them, taught marine skills to kids from fishing towns. Every student had to spend one day a month on a fishing panga. They threw huge nets over the water, dragged them in teeming with fish, and, back on shore, gutted and cleaned the catch before giving it to the town fishing cooperative for sale. Most of the kids despised working with fish and had to be forced by the system to go. But they went. Every month for three years, they went, for the good of the greater community that included some of their own families. Some of these teenagers went home to dirt floors and bare bulbs on the ceiling, with a hammock for a bed in an airless room they shared with a handful of relatives. I don't think one of my co-workers exaggerated when she described them as "so generous of spirit as to be almost noble."

Being around kids did my spirit good, too, but by 2002 Marsh needed my help at home.

Early in 1999, within a year of finishing Quinta Elena, neighbor Iberto had invited us to his annual birthday dinner party. An Italian businessman from Milan via Vancouver, Iberto had fussed as usual over a grand Italian meal for fifty or sixty of his local friends. It was a mild February evening, and we sat outside at tables and chairs arranged around a covered patio. Tea candles flickered at each table and music floated from the house through patio doors opened to the buffet table inside. Marsh was waiting his turn at the buffet and standing next to a man who introduced himself as Herman, a German medical doctor practicing in North Dakota and a sometime resident of Bucerias.

As Marsh recounted later, the doctor listened to him without comment as he told an abbreviated version of our move to Mexico, then pulled him out of line and out of earshot. Resting a hand on Marsh's arm, he said quietly, "You might not know this, but I am quite sure you have Parkinson's disease."

The doctor went on to list the symptoms he had observed: frozen facial muscles, slushy voice, the slightest of tremors in the right hand. Stunned, Marsh thanked him, excused himself, and came to find me.

"Please, El," he said, reaching for my glass, "let me freshen up that drink while I still can." He repeated what the doctor had just told him and added, "Really, his timing is so off, this is almost funny."

But it didn't seem funny when a neurologist confirmed the diagnosis five months later, during a summer stay in Austin with Marsh's daughters. She considered him to be in the intermediate stages of Parkinson's, a diagnosis seconded by a Parkinson's expert in Houston.

Both of us reacted to Parkinson's as we had reacted to prostate cancer—by acting quickly and stoically. We did an online search and read everything we found. I mailed off for brochures and books from the National Parkinson's Foundation, and we read some more. We bought a videotape of exercises for maintaining flexibility. We bought an audiotape of techniques for improving voice quality. We talked to people with Parkinson's and to friends of people with Parkinson's about what to expect.

From the onset, we felt hopeful. After all, Marsh was in good physical shape and experienced only a slight intermittent tremor in one hand. Even that stopped when he began medications. Together we would adhere to the medication schedule, do the flexibility exercises, and practice the voice techniques. Both Marsh and I believed what we had been told: More often than not, this disease progressed slowly, and patients had years, even decades, of active life after diagnosis. "That's going to be me," Marsh said with conviction.

It also dawned on us that Marsh's anxiety while crossing the Pacific had probably been Parkinson's-related. When the Houston expert prescribed Paxil and a small dose had a big effect, Marsh recognized the strain he had endured for three years. Blaming the disease for shortening the trip was convenient, true enough. But it relieved both of us from some of the guilt and resentment we had still harbored.

So, armed with resolve, medication, and a cartonful of books, pamphlets, and exercise tapes, we resumed life as we knew it. September through May, we were at home in Bucerias. But a sense of urgency tinged our life now, as if we knew the number of Marsh's remaining good days. We stopped putting off trips and hit the road in Mexico, as always without reservations or itineraries. We drove a grand loop of colonial cities, visiting Morelia, Cuernavaca, Puebla, Oaxaca, and Pátzcuaro. We returned to Oaxaca on a bus and stayed longer, taking in the surrounding villages and the ruins of Monte Alban, before heading south for Chiapas and its ruins at Palenque. On another bus trip, we beach-hopped up the Pacific coast, scouting the resort towns of Huatulco, Puerto Escondido, Acapulco, and Zihuatanejo.

Parkinson's didn't change Marsh's attitude toward travel and experiencing new places. He still wanted to go, especially for the first three years or so after the diagnosis. But the going was slower. His gait had changed to a tentative shuffle, and he held his hands in front of his body with fingers spread, as if braced for falls that didn't happen. He had to pace himself, so he took an afternoon nap for the first time in his adult life and could finally be talked out of hauling his own bags. "Part with the pesos and let some kid carry them," I said, pretending that money was the issue and not his loss of strength.

Stairs took a lot of energy, too. Marsh gripped handrails so tightly, his knuckles turned white when he pulled himself up the steps of the many old cathedrals and convents we visited. "Parkinson's feels like walking around in a concrete suit," one neurologist described it, and the effort Marsh had to make was obvious. And painful for me to watch.

I searched for more sedentary travel options that wouldn't take so much out of him. We attended the Cervantino festival in Guanajuato, the Pamplonada in San Miguel de Allende, and Marsh's favorite, the bullfights in Guadalajara to watch the Spanish nineteen-year-old phenomenon, "El Juli." Copper Canyon was our last long trip within Mexico; we rode a train deep into the canyon and stayed in rustic lodges along its route.

During June, July, and August, we headed for the border and out of the country, as we escaped the rain and steam heat. The drive was easy and after a dozen or more trips, we had the routine down. The first couple of years living in Mexico, we pushed on day one of the drive in order to make it as far as the same little one-motel town. As a lark, we always asked for the same room where, for $25, we got a sagging mattress, a lamp with no bulb, and sheets as soft as feed sacks. Now, because of Parkinson's, we stopped earlier and upgraded to a better motel. Marsh needed to get a good night's sleep. Even in our own bed, most nights he shot upright at least once, when muscles in his calves and toes spasmed, and he cried out to me to massage away the pain.

We changed motels but we didn't change the discussion we always had when we reached the border. Every year we bought three gift bottles of tequila for our daughters. Every year I insisted that no one would care if we were one over the legal limit of two, that it was almost silly to admit to such a petty crime, that it was easier to ask forgiveness than permission anyway. Marsh always nodded his agreement but never could manage the simple little lie. Every year he rolled down his window and confessed to the Border Patrol officer, who without fail smiled and waved us on through.

We crisscrossed the United States during most of those summers, and I did most of the driving. We stayed for a while with each of our kids and their families. We stopped in on brothers and sisters, nieces and nephews, old friends and a cousin or two. We often visited the same people during the summer who visited us in Mexico during the winter. "Swanning," we heard it called, this stopping to see people who had to take you in.

Or we would go a little farther. One year we rented a villa in Umbria and brought along some kids and grandkids to share it. Another year friend Kathy, now living in London, made all the arrangements and did all the driving during a swing through the Scottish Highlands and the English Lake District. Jennifer and Patrick had moved to Dublin, and for three summers, while Marsh was still able, we strolled the hills of Ireland with them and Pat's Irish family in Wicklow and Mayo.

The pilgrimage to Santiago de Compostela in Spain was one of Marsh's favorite summer trips. We drove the route used by the faithful for over a thousand years and, along with Lisa and her husband, Eddie, walked parts of the last one hundred miles to the medieval cathedral. Marsh rode as much as he walked, but he was happy. We could see it in his eyes, even beneath the Parkinson's "mask" that had begun to freeze the muscles in his face.

The two of us stayed on in Spain, so Marsh could treat me to the Festival of San Fermin in Pamplona, where he had once run with the bulls. As the young general manager of a new U.S. plant in Pamplona in the 1960s, he had been honored to run alongside the mayor. Together they sprinted ahead of the thundering herd and flailed at passing flanks with a rolled-up newspaper, before jumping a barricade to safety. The mayor later awarded him a pair of horns from one of that day's deceased, the same horns that now hung above our porch entrance at Quinta Elena.

We arrived for the last day of the festival and watched the running of the bulls from a beauty shop balcony. Later that afternoon, we headed for the ring, in search of scalped tickets for the sold-out bullfight.

"You're sure these tickets are for 'sombra' and not 'sol'?" Marsh asked the scalper.

"Absolutely," the scalper assured him. "Shadier than these seats, and you'll need earmuffs and cocoa."

We found our seats—in the brightest of "sol," where the afternoon sun blinded our eyes and blared down on our hatless, trusting heads.

Our neighbors didn't seem to mind, however. Unlike us, sitting empty-handed behind them, they uncorked champagne bottles and passed plates of shrimp before the first bull even entered the ring. Soon a man in a dapper ivy cap reached over his head with a tray of petit-fours and urged us to help ourselves.

"Welcome," he said, turning around in his seat. "I heard you speaking English—where are you from?" he asked.

"We're Americans," said Marsh in his best Castilian Spanish. "But I lived for three years in Pamplona thirty years ago and I'm happy to be back for the festival."

If San Fermín himself had risen from under Marsh's seat, the man could not have been more delighted. "Hijo mio! Our son has returned to us!" the man shouted to the people around him. "He's a Pamplonican, home at last. Get the man a glass."

Our bleacher neighborhood erupted in cheers of welcome and glasses raised to Marsh and his señora. A woman passed two glasses back to us, and men kept them filled with champagne the rest of the afternoon, while their wives circulated plates of savory and sweet tapas. People stood and offered toasts—to Marsh, to Spanish-U.S. relations, to peace and goodwill among mankind. We had landed in the middle of a crowd of locals, warming the same city-assigned seats every year and celebrating their biggest event of the year.

Plus we witnessed a grand day of bullfighting. Two toreros won ears that day, and the third was carried out the puerta grande on the shoulders of roaring fans. As we watched the torero's triumphant departure, we hooked arms and joined the thousands in the grand-stands as the crowd swayed in unison and sang chorus after chorus of "Pobre de mí," a lamentation to the close of Sanfermines for another year.

Like so many other summer getaways, this one had been fabulous. But it still felt great to be home when we swung through Quinta Elena's front gate in September. And nobody was happier to see us than our Labrador. Lola, who stayed behind with Michael most summers, would fly out the front door and crash-land at the base of the steps, skitter for traction on the cobblestones, then bolt toward Marsh. He braced himself on the gate as she ran into him, unable and unwilling to stop herself. With uncontainable glee, she bounced in front of him like Pluto on a pogo stick while he encouraged her, dangling the car keys under her nose and chanting, "Lola, Lola, Lola."

Always arriving after a long day of driving, we saved unpacking for the next day and instead grabbed a cold beer and made for the porch. We sat with our feet propped on the Equipal table and watched the sunset reflected in the swimming pool before us, Lola glued to Marsh's chair, her nose twitching as she sniffed the air of this olfactory paradise. It was good to be home and back to the mundane, or as Marsh often called it, "our lovely little life."

That was how he still saw it, in the early years after the Parkinson's diagnosis. He didn't seem to begrudge contracting the disease and mentioned often enough the Brown classmate in his twenty-fifth year with the disease who still sailed his boat single-handedly. Maybe he thought of it as cosmic justice, after his decades of good fortune: a comfortable, stable childhood with caring parents; a first-rate education in prestigious schools; an adulthood free of financial worry; children and stepchildren who loved and respected him; close friends scattered across the planet and dating back to high school. The kids and I demonstrated just how lovely his life had been in a video we made for his seventieth birthday. I had watched these retrospectives of a life before, at memorial services. I admired them, but wondered if the deceased had known just how terrific everyone seemed to think he was. Better Marsh should hear for himself.

Our son-in-law Patrick, an Intel engineer and self-taught video maker, volunteered to direct, and we went to work six months before Marsh's December birthday. Michael began by tweaking several dozen photos for a Web site. In a letter I sent to family and friends, I asked people to choose a photo and talk about it on an audiotape. They were to mail the audiotape, and any other photos or film they might like to include, to Pat and Jennifer in Dublin.

We code-named the secret project "Operation White Bear." Letters, e-mails, photographs, audiotapes, video clips, and music files flew back and forth across oceans for months, bearing witness to the affection people felt for Marsh. He suspected nothing, despite one close call during our stay in Dublin that summer. An audiotape arrived from Australia, with the return address of M. Oddie hand-printed on the mailer. Marsh noticed the postmark when he saw the mailer on the kitchen table and picked it up.

"Hey, how come you're getting mail from our friend Michael Oddie?" asked Marsh, calling to Jennifer, who sat in the next room reading the *Irish Times*.

Jennifer didn't miss a beat. She put down the paper, came into the kitchen, took the mailer from Marsh, and pretended to study it.

"Oh, this is from Mark Oddie, a rugby buddy of Pat's from the Old Blues," she said. "He moved to Melbourne a couple of years ago." This seemed to satisfy Marsh, but she took the mailer with her anyway as she left the kitchen.

Pat and Jennifer spent hundreds of hours compiling, editing, and hunting for material on the Internet. The finished product was brilliant, as was the response rate of people asked to participate—95 percent came through for us. Marsh watched the tape many times over the next years. I caught him a few times, late at night when he couldn't sleep, in front of the TV, smiling as he watched the tape. After a trying day with Parkinson's, it consoled him, he said, to remember the love that surrounded him and to be reminded of his more than fair share of glory days.

We featured the video during a weekend-long celebration. Mariachis kicked off Friday night, after first hiding in the lower garden and waiting for the signal that Marsh's sisters, kids, and friends had all assembled by the pool. Dressed in silver-studded black, the eight musicians strolled up Alberto's pool house steps playing the Mexican birthday serenade, "Las Mañanitas." Lisa, Marilyn, Kathy, and I made the food—heavy hors d'oeuvres and Marsh's favorite spice cake shaped into a seven and a zero. The next night, after a family dinner on the beach at the elegant Casa Las Brisas, an unsuspecting Marsh returned to Quinta Elena, where Jennifer and Michael had set up a TV and rings of chairs in the living room.

"We couldn't find your favorite movies, Marsh—no *Patton* or *Shrek* in all of Puerto Vallarta," said Jennifer. "So we're showing this one instead."

Surrounded by his family and close friends, Marsh watched the opening photos of himself as a kid in Barrington, Rhode Island. He heard his father singing in the background as Ray led the Brown University men's glee club in an a cappella rendition of "Captain McGee." All eyes were on him, and when his chin began to quiver, we broke into laughter and applause.

People had taped great stories. They talked about his hauling fondue pots to the top of Mount Wachusett for late-afternoon suppers. They sent clips of him swallowing a torch of fire as he marched in the Northborough Fourth of July parade. His old friend Dick told about their Saturday night couples card games. All of them were young marrieds at the time, with babies and no extra money for sitters. In a precursor to baby monitors, Marsh came up with the idea of wiring microphones over the cribs of the sleeping babies and running them to speakers at the home of the Saturday night hosts.

One night the eight card players were horrified to hear heavy breathing from the speaker wired to the Greenes' house. Bent on saving baby Lisa from the intruder, the men dashed to the garage, grabbed baseball bats, and tore across three lawns, to find Barry, the family's one-hundred-fifty-pound St. Bernard, standing with his nose pressed into the mike.

But bullfights in Pamplona and seventieth birthdays are highlights of a life, good material for annual holiday letters. They don't reflect the day to day. Marsh's days had become slower as his Parkinson's advanced. He tired easily. Taking Lola for their early-morning walk on the beach exhausted him, and was soon impossible when, by 2002, he no longer had the strength to climb our hill. His falling asleep at the table became the norm during dinner parties. He had also given up driving in 2002, unable to react quickly or to judge distances accurately or to control the frequent gushes of tears, caused by dry eyes with lids that "forgot" to blink.

Two nasty falls on the tennis court ended the last sport Marsh was able to play and a lifetime of athletics; his scared partner, Luis, brought him home covered in blood from forehead and leg wounds. He was losing eye-hand coordination quickly: He cut his fingers when slicing or dicing, missed the glass when pouring, and made a mess when painting or varnishing. So he couldn't help me much in the kitchen, make his Perfect

Margaritas, or paint the black grillwork and varnish the window frames after the rainy season ended. The fact that he rarely complained made it all the more poignant to watch him shuffling aimlessly from room to room, searching unsuccessfully for things to fix or ways to help out.

"I feel watt-less," he said, after a long day of too little activity.

Even more upsetting, for Marsh and for me, was his rapid mental decline. By early 2001, we knew he was among the unlucky Parkinson's patients also afflicted with dementia. Unlike Alzheimer's, Parkinson's dementia is described as "loss of executive reasoning," its victims fully aware of what they are losing. This man, who could multiply three numbers by three numbers in his head, now couldn't move a decimal point to figure out a 10 percent tip. He couldn't order the sequence of events for the Navy stories he had told dozens of times. And he had begun to hallucinate, first miniature people and animals, but by 2003, normal-sized people he talked to and followed around the house.

The motion specialist in Austin had warned me early on to expect the hallucinations.

"With most patients, they are benign, nonthreatening figures who come and go quickly," he said.

He adjusted and readjusted the various meds in attempts to reduce the number of their appearances, but

because they never frightened Marsh, we eventually
gave up and instead learned to live with these uninvited
guests. The two of us even kidded about them.

"How many for dinner tonight, Marsh?" I'd ask.

"I don't know; they won't give me a final count," he'd
answer, as even now he made fun of himself, then softened the accusation with his familiar tag line: "It just
makes me furious," he said.

## "Remember the Sweet Things"

· his slicing and dicing for hours, while we make
dinner for guests; his praising the cook and waving off
any credit for his part

· his dining room candelabra tutorials: asking
people to help him lower it from the cupola, light the
candles, hoist it up again, and clean it off; lots of bonus
chatter about the potential for disaster

· his rolling on the floor with three-month-old
Lola, nuzzling her and speaking baby talk

· his putting in twelve-hour workdays for a week, knocking off the projects on a list I'd given him, getting ready for a party

· his enthusiasm about going anywhere, anytime, to check out anything we haven't experienced before

· he and Jennifer, forehead to forehead, harmonizing on "Her Mother Never Told Her"

· the lovely predictability of being met at the airport by my smiling partner, delighted to see me

· saying, "I missed you at dinner" because he was seated far down the table and we couldn't talk to each other

· buying me a bouquet of bright orange dried corn husk "flowers" for Mother's Day because Bucerias doesn't have a flower shop

· driving around and around in downtown Puerto Vallarta, looking for a restaurant whose address I hadn't written down, with no grousing or trying to make me feel guilty

· between guest visits, enjoying our self-containment

and our routine: *The News Hour,* dinner, a movie, and good night

• his return from Sunday tennis with Pancho, Luis, and El Profe, dripping with sweat, energized, greeting Lola with a hearty "Hi, pup."

• my criticizing his bed making, telling him the decorative pillows were placed too deliberately; next morning, his making the bed and tossing on the pillows from five feet away, saying, "Now that bed looks inviting, don't you think?"

• coming home after midnight, both of us dog tired; sitting up a while longer with a nightcap to debrief the evening

• in Austin, after two weeks of tests and doctors' visits; lying in bed, holding hands, numbed by the diagnosis of Parkinson's disease

• feeling like doofuses, renting a cottage on tiny Silver Lake, Wisconsin, and pedaling around in a pontoon boat each evening at sunset; "Ma and Pa Kettle do a circumnavigation," he said.

• on the road with Kathy in Scotland, stopping for

the night at first-class castles-cum-hotels; playing a savage round of croquet at a pitch on the Isle of Bute

&bull; the millennium at Quinta Elena: dinner for twelve for ten nights, with a rotation of cooks turning out ex-travaganzas; an arduous, dusty day trip to San Sebastian; waking up baby Lily to bring her to the beach at midnight; being surrounded by people we love for two solid weeks

&bull; MARSH: Whistling in the kitchen while putting
 away dishes from the dishwasher
 ELLEN: "What's that you're whistling?"
 MARSH: "The refrain from 'The Dance of the
 Nubian Slave Girls.'"
 ELLEN: "Of course."

&bull; the inadvertently all-orange dinner he fixed for Mike and Priscilla, while I was gone for Anna's birth—salmon, carrots, saffron rice, and sherbet

&bull; Lisa and I forcing him to buy $200 walking shoes; his grousing at the price and saying, "You two better promise to bury me in these shoes."

&bull; on his hands and knees, next to the pool with Lola, his face in the water, demonstrating how to bob for the tennis balls she'd lost there

• in bed, spotting a huge hairy brown spider above us on the ceiling; slowly crawling up my back with his fingertips, slapping his hands next to my ear, pretending to kill it

• the three-day round of parties to celebrate his seventieth: his being surprised at the airport by his sisters and five kids; mariachis around the pool and margaritas by the gallon; a sunset on the beach and cubanos after dinner at Casa Las Brisas; the video à la Ken Burns, celebrating his life

• riding bikes in County Cork; his slow-motion pratfall into a hedge

• his belting out the Brown fight song while we watched the Rose Bowl

• his buying a straw hat in Tzintzuntzan and always wearing it to the airport, hoping people will notice so he can tell them where he got it

• my torn knee ligaments on the mend after a fall on the street; his impatience with me when I tried to help myself: "Call me!" "I'll do that!" "Go sit down!"

• his tenderness with Lola, carrying her back and

forth to the vet when she had her close call with para-
sites; talking softly to her at night in the study, after her
days at the vet's on an IV

 • his Christmas cookie decorating, still long on
enthusiasm, short on aesthetics; the aerial sprinkling
"technique" he uses to get a rise out of me

 • his annual holiday tradition with Jennifer: listening to the CD of him and the Salisbury Singers singing "Adeste Fidelis," looking at each other sheepishly,
breaking into tears during the big finish, and consoling
each other with a hug

 • his sitting on the porch with baby Lily, entertaining her with finger-pulling games; two years later, sitting on the same porch, this time with baby Annie in
his lap, both asleep with chin on chest

 • driving the pilgrimage to Santiago de Compostela; treating ourselves to paradores; chewing on hard
sausage and crusty bread in O'Cebreiro; oohing and
aahing with the throng of pilgrims in the cathedral as
the giant incense burner swung over our heads

# Chapter 8

## *Living with Parkinson's:*
## *1999–2006*

MARSH SAT ON OUR FRONT PORCH, READING HIS
book or staring out to sea for hours, as Parkinson's took
over his body and his mind. From the beginning, he
accepted his lot with few complaints. I never heard him
ask anything resembling "Why me?" No one remem-
bers his offering an unsolicited description of his pain
and suffering. He would have called it "whining." If
pressed, he might state a few facts, but he rarely tacked
on the feelings connected to them. So he might share
that his fingers were too stiff for a keyboard, without
adding how much he missed writing his own e-mails.
With most people, he skipped any particulars and stuck
to vague generalities. "I have good days and bad days,"
he would say.

As Marsh's caregiver, I think I would have preferred
more complaining. I felt a surge of empathy any time

he shared his sadness or frustration. We were in this together and I wanted to be inside that concrete suit he wore, feeling what he was feeling, so I could find more ways to relieve his burden. It was lonely, watching from the outside. People make it sound like high praise to call their partner "low maintenance." If they mean their partner doesn't share much, doesn't engage much, doesn't speak up much about personal needs, then I don't find it all that praiseworthy. Taking care of my sick husband was my most important job now, and I needed to be needed. But he had so little practice expressing negative feelings that the vocabulary was buried deep.

*You seem down today, Marsh. Are you?*
*A little, I guess.*
*How come?*
*Oh, nothing special.*
*No, really. Tell me.*
*I didn't sleep too well last night.*
*Why not?*
*Hard to say.*
*Were you worried about something?*
*Maybe that was it.*

"I feel like a dentist," I shouted at him more than once as I tried to yank the words out of his mouth.

His opening up would have helped with some practicalities, too. For us, Parkinson's was all about tinkering with medications. Powerful medications that could stop the wild gyrating of his hips and create phantoms who stood next to his chair. We worked with a motion specialist in Austin and a neurologist in Vallarta, both of whom relied on me for anecdotal evidence on how Marsh's Parkinson's was progressing (the "progress" of a disease. A curious word choice, if you think of progress as positive. So getting worse is a good thing?). They adjusted dosages and changed the cocktail of pills every other visit, based on what I told them was happening at home. For me, having to rely more on my own observations than on input from Marsh, it seemed like dismaying guesswork.

In the beginning, we were sloppy about pill taking, and that didn't help us track progress. I had never seen Marsh take so much as an aspirin tablet—his never suffering from a hangover, no matter the excess, had always been a mixed blessing. Now he took a fistful of pills every four hours to treat rigidity, dyskinesia, hallucinations, depression, and anxiety. Like most PWPs (for People with Parkinson's) and their caregivers, we moved through stages. First, Marsh filled his seven pill containers, carried one in his pocket every day, and tried to remember to take the pills on time. When he made too many mistakes filling the container compartments, I filled them. When he missed too many doses, we bought him an alarm watch to help him remember. When the dementia advanced to the point that he stared at the watch and couldn't relate the time on the watch to the times written on the compartments, I wore the alarm watch. Finally, when Marsh took the wrong pills by confusing the compartments or leaving some pills behind, I carried the day's container and handed him the pills.

I remember the afternoon we decided it was time for me to carry the containers. It was no small thing, Marsh's not being able to open the right box and empty it, boxes marked in big numbers with 8 A.M., 12, 4 P.M., and 8 P.M. We sat on the sofa in the study, where he rested his head in my lap and I stroked his hair.

"I feel humiliated," Marsh said.

"It's not your fault, you know," I said.

"I know," he said.

A quiet moment passed, after which he broke my heart. "I wish I could be smart again for you," he said.

It had taken us four years to arrive at this stage, and it had been a bumpy road. Marsh's slippage had been uneven, which kept us off balance. One day he could offer an opinion on the war in Afghanistan, for example, after watching the television news. The next he couldn't follow the storyline of a straightforward movie like *Cats and Dogs*. He could put an exercise tape into the VCR and turn on the TV one week, then be confused about how to open the tape box the next. Watching Marsh set the table for a dinner party reflected the chaos in his mind: Some evenings, he would move quickly around the table, putting knives, forks, and spoons beside the plates in their normal places; other evenings, he would put a knife and fork to the right of one plate, a lone fork to the right of another, two spoons and a knife around a third. My impatient correcting of the place settings must have deflated him at the time; I feel ashamed of myself now whenever I think about it.

Marsh continued to handle the mechanics of our life well after I should have taken over the job. I fooled myself into believing he was still up to bill paying and house maintenance: first, because I disliked the jobs he had always done so well; and second, because I was loath to take anything more away from him. So he forgot to renew the car insurance and registration. Checks he had written came back because he hadn't made them out to anyone. We drank unpurified water because the cartridge wasn't replaced. The car didn't get oil and filter changes. Lola didn't get her rabies shot. The portfolio was ignored. So were the bank trust and property taxes on our house; by the time I acted, we were two years in arrears.

Maybe both of us were in denial. Maybe we were like most people and dealt with the unpleasant only when forced. Or more likely, maybe we simply were not sure of how much Marsh could or couldn't do. In any event, I came out of the fog and faced the reality of our life with Parkinson's when he missed a flight to Houston.

I had driven him to the Vallarta airport and asked permission to walk him to his gate for the direct flight. The Vallarta airport was still small in 2002, and exceptions to rules still possible. As always, Marsh was anxious about flying and wanted to arrive early, so even after killing time over soup and salad, he had an hour's wait before takeoff. We passed through security, went to Gate 2, and sat in the only row facing it.

"You don't need to wait. Go ahead, you have things to do and I have my book," Marsh said. So I took off. But he didn't—he never got on his plane. A Mexican agent noticed him sitting where I left him and put him on another flight a few hours later. "He's all right," said his son, Jeff, when he finally reached me at home. He had waited in Houston for the next flight from Vallarta and met Marsh as planned. "He's a little dazed and can't understand what might have happened, but said to tell you not to be concerned."

Concerned? I was mortified. At some level, I knew I should never have left Marsh alone. But more devastating than that was the clear-eyed look I now had at our future. Marsh was not going to be among those whom doctors and friends told us about so often. His disease was not going to progress slowly. He was not going to have years of active life ahead. It wasn't going to matter how religiously he worked with the hand weights we bought or did the muscle-stretching and voice-strengthening exercises in the books and videos we ordered. I could continue to read "Ask the Doctor" online every day and follow the suggestions from other PWPs. I could whip up protein powder malts by the gallon and high-fiber oatmeal cookies by the gross and prune-raisin paste by the bucketfuls. None of it would alter the course of what was happening to Marsh's mind.

That wasn't all. As if dementia weren't enough, a new condition was developing. Two disks in Marsh's spine had disintegrated, and pieces of stray bone now pressed on nerves, which shot pain up and down his left side. The pain crippled him; he could stand for only minutes at a time and moaned in his sleep when he tried to turn his body. We tried cortisone shots, acupuncture, then back surgery. Nothing worked. The pain was excruciating, and we fought it for three years, frantic for relief, before resorting to a pain-management program of still more pills and more tinkering until we hit on the right formula.

Pain, pills, and Parkinson's sapped Marsh's strength, so we cut back on socializing and spent more and more time at home. We took to arriving late and leaving early from the big buffet supper affairs that were popular among expats in Bucerias. We accepted few invitations to restaurants, preferring to invite to our house the select few who didn't mind if the host spilled a sloshing drink or needed a hand with buttering his roll.

I told Marsh that I preferred evenings at home alone. "It's always been our way, enjoying our own company the most," I said. I wasn't being heroic. I had begun to picture myself without him, craving him, longing to have him back and all to myself. I was practicing how to be a widow.

Soon the get-togethers with anyone other than family and close friends became more trying than enjoyable. Marsh's soft, slushy voice had deteriorated to the point he couldn't make himself understood in a crowd. My repeating what he had said just embarrassed him. So he resigned himself to sitting silently, and the group gradually ignored him as the evening wore on. It wasn't that people were unkind. It was just too taxing, this straining to hear him and to include him.

Marsh came up with a ploy to include himself in the conversation. He practiced one-liners in his head, simple phrases he could interject during a lull, when he stood a chance of being heard. Mostly his favorite old sayings that didn't call for a response—he couldn't feel sure he'd be clever enough to field a comeback.

"Beats a sharp stick in the eye," he might say, a beat too late, or "Hoist by your own petard," off the mark yet obscure enough to slip by the listeners. But he recognized how ridiculous he sometimes sounded. On our way home one night, he stared out the car window and, in a rare moment of candor, said, "I miss being the funny one."

I ached for him. He knew when people laughed too hard at his smallest comment and made too much of his most innocuous observation. He detested it when casual acquaintances took his hand in both of theirs and asked him oh so earnestly how he was doing. It jolted him one evening, at the end of a dinner party, when a woman held him too long in a goodbye hug, then turned away, overcome by emotion.

"Am I that bad?" he asked me, from the safety of our car. He knew the answer, and his eyes filled with tears.

I was furious with all those who patronized him. "They mean well," Marsh said. But I wanted to shriek at them. See this man hanging on my arm and shuffling toward a chair? He got us into Hiva Oa after twenty-five days at sea. This confused man who can't tell you his phone number? He could work the figures and tell you if China or India would be the best place for your factory. This poker-faced man in the Parkinson's mask who scares kids on planes when he tries to chat them up? He used to round up his friends' kindergartners to come celebrate his birthday with hot dogs and cupcakes.

I was so angry. Damn the well-heeled friends who didn't make the time to come see him. The same for healthy relatives who saw us only when the sick one came to them. And what good were the open-ended invitations to faraway ski houses and sailboats if they required hours of preparation and complicated travel, just so Marsh could sit and watch other people do the things he had enjoyed so much? Long after putting him to bed, I would hide in the study, drinking too much rum and railing at them in letters that got thrown away in the morning.

I was angry with Marsh, too. He wasn't trying. He would rally for visits with his kids and tell the occasional story to close friends who gave him the time to feel comfortable. But for the most part he sat on the porch with his book and made no effort to keep up with activities to help himself, like playing cards for finger dexterity or singing out loud for voice strength. When asked if he would like to listen to music or an audiobook, he would say yes, but he never asked first. If I suggested he join me in the pool for water aerobics, he refused as often as he accepted. Two medications had failed to touch his depression, and apathy was overtaking him. His kids were stunned. "In the fifty years I've known Dad, I don't ever remember seeing him depressed or bored, until now," said Lisa, during one of her frequent visits.

"This is so unlike you," I yelled at him and pounded the steering wheel as we drove into Vallarta on errands. "You can't give up like this. You have to give a damn."

It was for show. In the past, angry chiding had made him try harder, at least for a few days. Now I didn't believe what I was saying—I had given up, too, and was probably only a little less depressed than Marsh. And scared. In the past month, he had tripped and fallen several times in Vallarta, twice in the middle of a busy street. Each time his body twisted into an awkward position from which I couldn't pull him up, and strangers had hurried over to help me. Blood ran down his arms and legs as we limped down crowded streets, Marsh draping his good arm around my shoulder and me waving off offers of assistance as I looked wild-eyed for a restaurant and a ladies' room where I could clean him up. Now every time he stumbled on the cobblestones and uneven sidewalks, my heart lurched and I cursed out loud.

Something had to change. We might have many years to go with Parkinson's and spending them in this angry, fearful, hopeless frame of mind was untenable. Both of us needed to change our focus—not on what the disease was destroying, but on what we ourselves could still create. And the way to make that change was staring us in the face.

Two years after the completion of Quinta Elena, we had come home in September to the surprise of an unimaginative, three-story condominium going up next door and towering over our pool. Heartsick, we reacted by shopping for another piece of land and found a beauty about twenty minutes north, in the even smaller town of San Francisco. Nicknamed San Pancho, the town had been transformed into a kind of model village in the 1970s by a former Mexican president and had maintained its appeal. We bought a hillside lot with gorgeous views of the sea, the sierra, and the jungle around us.

But we couldn't decide what to do with the property. For two years, we agonized over the pros and cons of building another house. The biggest negatives packed mental and physical wallops: Moving out of a house he loved might be asking too much of Marsh emotionally; building another might be too taxing for him to participate and thus could do him more harm than good.

Yet the positives for building again were just as powerful. We needed a project to give us a sense of purpose, and we needed the tidy profit from a sale of Quinta Elena in order to reline our coffers. When I took over our finances, I was shocked to learn how much value our portfolio had lost in the last few years and how little cash it could generate. Now we depended mainly on Marsh's Social Security and pension checks; without him, they disappeared or were cut by a third. The bottom line: I couldn't afford to live at Quinta Elena as a widow without going back to work. And how old would I be when I went looking for a job?

That settled it for Marsh. "The important thing is to

secure your future," he said. "And that means with some raisins in your oatmeal, too."

"Would you enjoy building another house?" I asked.

"That doesn't matter. Your enjoying it is what matters now," he answered.

After all the agonizing, the decision to build in San Pancho seemed obvious once we made it. But it only turned out to be the right decision because of Marsh's attitude. He couldn't do much to help me get the house ready for sale, or to pack and move out of it, or to find and move into Casa Indalo, a rental house in San Pancho. However, he was my uncomplaining partner every step of the way, who supported me with praise and verbal shoulder rubs at the end of long days.

I know it hurt him to watch me do most of the work. This was a man who, more than anything else, lived to please others. He was the one who could load up the cars after a group getaway, hauling out bags and strapping on skis without being in the way. He was the guest who could find the sheets to change a bed and the scrub pad to wash dirty pots without a barrage of questions. He could turn out a tasty dish without the flurry of officiousness or the thinly veiled demand for compliments of so many male cooks.

It devastated Marsh when Parkinson's made it impossible for him to be of use to others. "I hate being a burden," he said, through gritted teeth and angry tears. It didn't mean he hated being helped; it meant he hated not helping. I tried to involve him in the packing and moving. But he probably wasn't fooled by the feather-light boxes of unbreakables I asked him to carry.

He didn't say anything, however. Nor did he object to long meetings with architect Carolina in which he had nothing to offer and was ignored altogether when we got down to business. Often he fell asleep while she and I dickered over details. I would wake him up to walk him into the bedroom, lay him down to swing his legs across the bed, and give him a quick kiss on the forehead. In return, he would smile, squeeze my hand, and thank me, and his gallantry would bring a lump to my throat.

How I loved this dear man; what tenderness I felt for him. Before his very eyes, Parkinson's had stolen his passion for life, and for me. I felt the loss keenly and sometimes ached for his caress. But the disease couldn't take away his thoughtfulness or make me doubt his de-votion to me. Knowing this to be true had to be enough for me, and it was.

While Marsh didn't play an active role in the design or construction of Quinta Elena II, he enjoyed a daily visit to the site. As with the previous crew, the masons and their helpers liked to see us on-site and to chat with us. He had lost his ability to speak Spanish—he struggled to find words in English now, but couldn't find them at all in Spanish or Chinese. So it was up to the crew to approach him, which the senior men did freely. Every day they greeted him with hearty hellos and asked what he thought of his fine new house. They took him by the arm and slowly steered him over to look at a feature they thought would impress him: porch rails lashed together with jungle vines; a ceiling of red bricks arched over the kitchen, a bathroom floor made of sea stones, set into concrete, pebble by pebble.

"¿Que tal, Don Marshall?" they asked, all smiles. "What do you think?" And he would answer by giving a thumbs-up.

Four of the masons came to our job from Guanajuato and lived at the site. They slept on cots in the small outbuilding already on the property and cooked simple food over an open fire. A pot of beans was always simmering, and eggshells lay scattered around the fire, along with dried-out tortillas that Lola liked to root for, her snout coated with soot. She loved hanging out with the guys. They called her Lolita and pitched her tortillas like Frisbees, which she leaped high in the air to catch. The house we rented was only a few hundred meters from the site and an easy walk for Lola, down rutted country roads, old cobblestones pried loose by heavy rains. It made us laugh to watch our dog in black face, bouncing back up the lane, her belly swaying with tortilla snacks.

The construction progressed smoothly and according to schedule; Casa Indalo was comfortable for the duration. But I was anxious to settle us in the new house. Marsh had lost some ground over the nine-month process. He could still feed himself, but it was a trial. He didn't have the strength to spear pieces of meat nor the teeth to chew them—four had broken or fallen out, in a mouth already a mess and calling for dentures. His depth of vision was deteriorating, too, so he missed when reaching for his glass, and his fork came up empty after repeated stabs at his plate. We showered together now so I could help him, and I dressed him, his torso too stiff to pull on shorts and a shirt, his fingers too rigid to do up buttons and zippers. He took a two-hour nap in the morning, another in the afternoon, slept for ten hours a night, and still fell asleep over his book or while watching TV, which indicated a worsening of the dementia.

It was dangerous now for him to be alone. He forgot instructions about not cooking unless I was with him and left burners on and freezer doors open. During a visit with Jennifer and Pat in California, he lost his bearings when out for a walk he promised would only be to the corner and back. The kids and I circled the neighborhood in cars until we found him a few blocks away with a concerned woman who had called the police when Marsh couldn't explain where Jennifer lived. The three of them were trying to figure out how to get him home when Michael happened by. From then on, I put a note in his pocket, with address and phone number.

The last time I left him alone, I had run into the village for eggs while Marsh was napping one afternoon, and returned to find him gone. After a check around the house and garden, I jumped in the car and drove to the top of the site. No, said the guys, who had knocked off for the day and were seated around their fire with plates of food, they hadn't seen him. We spread out over the hilltop and shouted Marsh's name but received no response, other than to excite Lola. She had shown up as usual when the beans and tortillas were being served. Now she picked up on our nervousness, we thought, and raced up and down the hill between us and the new construction site.

Afraid, I got back in the car and headed for the village one more time, traversing the streets Marsh might have taken and getting out to walk the stretch of beach between Casa Indalo and the town center. It was deserted, and I saw no one in the water. I crept back to the rental, peering down every alleyway, and ran into the house calling his name. No answer. Then I drove back to the site to pick up the crew—they could serve as a posse and fan out across the area to look for him while enough daylight remained to spot him. My little Toyota charged up the hill and sent up a cloud of dust when

I braked hard in front of the crew, gathered around Marsh.

The short, dark-skinned Guanajuato masons stood behind Marsh, who sat on an overturned five-gallon paint can, dusty and bleeding from cuts on his knees. Each of the men had a hand resting on Marsh's shoulder and wore a solemn expression, as if positioned for a tintype from the Old West captioned "Comanches with captive."

Marsh insisted he was okay—he was covered with blood and dirt, but there were no broken bones. He said Lola had found him. After his nap, he had gone looking for her. He fell while climbing the hill, then rolled down to the new house, where he remained pinned in a corner. He couldn't pull himself up or call out loudly enough to be heard by anyone but her. Lola dashed up and down between him and all of us, stopping only long enough to give his wounds a quick lick, until someone paid attention to her and followed her down to Marsh.

The next morning when I arrived at the site, I saw something new. A rough bridge ran across the hill and down to the construction site. The masons had cobbled it together from pieces of scaffolding and built it by the light of the moon; now they were adding handrails as the finishing touch. They waved off my thanks, as if this act of kindness were nothing out of the ordinary. But when I brought Marsh to admire it the following day, they gathered around him to witness a test walk, shouted their approval when he made it across, and declared it the Marshall Greene Memorial Bridge.

I want to think that building Quinta Elena II was as good for Marsh as it was for me. I know our improved finances and rosier future pleased him. We made a 200 percent profit on the sale of the Bucerias house, beefed up our portfolio, and built an even nicer house in a more desirable location. I also know that he benefited from my upgrade in attitude as the San Pancho place took shape and we had something positive to show for soldiering on through difficult days. For me, it felt normal again—to be in motion, to be in control, acting rather than reacting.

This is not to say I never again reacted too harshly or judged too critically or cried myself to sleep thinking about a bleak future. But by May 2005, when we moved into the new place, I had evolved into a calmer, more caring caregiver. Other caregivers will probably understand when I say that this was due in part to Marsh's needs becoming constant. When assured of what he needed, I could deliver it. And I could resign myself to the new level of need. Surprises caused the spiritual nosedives, not the day-to-day regimen of helping Marsh.

So the first time he held up a checkout line at a crowded store, unable to pay because he couldn't get his cramped fist out of his pocket and then couldn't differentiate the bills he fingered, I was flustered and didn't know what to do. From then on, I made sure I stood ahead of him in line with my wallet in hand. The first time I found him on the porch, staring at the page of a book he was holding upside down, I closed my eyes tight to hold back the tears. So Michael bought him headphones and we moved on to audiobooks. When he took the Mini mental status exam and scored 16 out of 22, not able, for instance, to write a sentence or repeat "no ifs, ands, or buts," both of us were despondent. After that, we didn't bother with tests that only verified the obvious.

My outlook, and therefore my caregiving, also improved when I stopped thinking of Marsh and Ellen Greene as the center of the universe. Why had I expected others to hustle down to Mexico more often than they did? They had kids and grandkids and urgencies of their own. Marsh wasn't terminally ill. And I hadn't made any heroic efforts to reach out during others' time of need— what gave me the nerve to be pointing a finger now?

If I were a caring caregiver at all, it had little to do with extraordinary bigness of spirit on my part. Plain and simple, Marsh had earned it. He had made regular deposits of graciousness and kindness into an account he could now draw on and pay in full for the good treatment he deserved.

Neither had he brought any of his health problems on himself. He had always played active sports, eaten well, kept his weight down, and gone for physicals. He didn't smoke. He drank in moderation. I am not sure how I would have dealt with a spouse whose own excesses created a burden I was forced to bear.

I could also feel calm and self-confident about caregiving because we had the safety net of good health care coverage. As a twenty-year veteran of the U.S. Navy Reserves, Marsh was eligible for a new federal program called TRICARE for LIFE. A free supplemental plan, it included drug coverage that reduced the cost of his medications from thousands of dollars to a few hundred. For six years, I had been reading the National Parkinson's Foundation website, "Ask the Doctor," and heard about many other PWPs who were not so lucky. "I give thanks to a grateful nation," Marsh kidded, but he spoke the truth.

And we lived in Mexico, where we could find and afford at-home help. Not only in Mexico but in San Pancho, a quiet little town that was home to a regional hospital. How perfect, we thought. We had already found Ana, who did such an efficient, caring job, helping him in and out of bed, making him meals, and goading him into cleaning his plate. When the time came, we would look for affordable hospital workers to provide more comprehensive home health care. That was our plan.

If you want to make God laugh, tell him your plans—isn't that how the old saw goes?

# "Remember the Sweet Things"

• the reunion in Shanghai; his old staff crowding around him, hanging on his every word; Xiao Li's artful scheduling of banquets, time at his lavish new apartment, and rest; Xiao Zhao's exuberance while driving around his favorite "big potato"

• his walking past Jennifer, the jumbo sack of pills under his arm, and laughing when she said, "Just say no, Elvis."

• driving anyone and everyone up to our lot in San Pancho; reveling in their first awestruck take on the spectacular view

• at the Coyote Lodge overlooking Copper Canyon, huddled under three layers of wool blankets

• picking grapefruit for breakfast in the garden of Casa Indalo

• our first sunset and "hora feliz" on the front porch of Quinta Elena II

• his happy problem of Lisa and Jen's vying for him as their houseguest when he comes to Austin

• the infamous Ride to Ruidoso: twenty hours in the car for an hour of skiing with Jen and his grandkids, with no complaints from him and lots of laughs

• Jennifer's calling him "Old Man" and chiding him: "Old Man, don't make me come over there and force-feed you those pancakes."

• Lola sitting at his feet in the bathroom, staring up at him while he shaves, cocking her head as if judging how well he's doing

• his being anxious about having Christmas and birthday gifts for me now that he can't drive; his arranging shopping trips with daughters to help him get something I'd like

• his spending hours on the porch with each of his children as they come, one by one, to be with him awhile

• ELLEN: "Thanks for putting up with leftovers for dinner again tonight."
  MARSH: "First a gourmet meal, then gourmet leftovers—I've got it made."

• the old joke with "Nurse Lisa": after telling her that he's having a good day, adding the faux plea for sympathy, "But you know I'm still very sick."

• his raving as usual about the Christmas fruitcake made only for him

• his picking a pink bougainvillea blossom from out front and placing it on my pillow

• his giving Chava, the carpenter, the gift of his father's planer; Chava's stroking it, choked up and misty-eyed

• always the gentleman, thanking me time after time for buttoning his shirt or cutting his food or helping him shave

• agreeing that when we meet in another lifetime, he will slip "Fort Sumter" into the conversation so I'll recognize him

• telling me that he considers it a little gift each time that he wakes up and finds himself being held by me

# Chapter 9

## *Leave-taking:*
## *June 2006*

BY THE END OF 2005, MARSH'S DAYS WERE INDEED "watt-less." He no longer had the eye-hand coordination or the mental agility to scroll down on a computer, turn on a TV with a remote, or place a phone call. Listening to an audiobook put him to sleep within minutes; so did riding in the car. His voice was so soft, his speech so slurred, that most of what he said to me had to be repeated, which annoyed both of us and resulted in his making less and less of an effort to speak. Down to 140 pounds, he had little appetite and would have been happy to subsist on protein powder ice cream shakes.

Marsh drifted through his days, unable to understand the things happening to him or around him. You could see the confusion in his eyes, hear it in the questions he asked. Anything out of the ordinary threw him; travel was especially incomprehensible. When we flew to San Jose, California, for Christmas with Jennifer, Pat, and the girls that year, we went over the travel plan every day for a week: which day we were leaving; what we would pack for him; where we would take Lola; what time we should arrive at the airport; how long we were staying. Yet every day he woke up and asked, "Is this the day we leave?" Or "Who are we staying with?" Or "Why are we going to California?" It was not unlike talking to a toddler, who trusts the answers being given, but either can't remember them from the day before or takes comfort from the repetition.

Marsh's questioning abated, however, as his apathy increased. More and more, he lost interest in the goings-on around him. He said it was all the same to him if he did or didn't listen to a book, go out for lunch, or visit with friends. Frankly, I was relieved. Not only was I tired of inventing activities for him that he didn't care about or resisted, but he now appeared less anxious, more tranquil. Friends who met him for the first time in Mexico had often described him as sweet and gentle; now I agreed with them. Before Parkinson's, that description wouldn't have suited him at all. To be sure, he had always been thoughtful and a gentleman. But my Marsh was also high energy and gutsy, quick-witted and competitive. To have known only the sick Marsh was to have missed knowing the Pied Piper who swept you up with his good cheer and took you along on adventures that made you feel zany and special.

That Marsh was the one our kids remembered when they came to visit, staggering their stays so one of them was in San Pancho every month. They came individually to ensure enough time for meaningful talk on the porch with their father and stepfather. They knew he did better with one-on-one conversation—it was easier for him to hear and to process. They also knew he was losing the ability to converse with them at all.

His kids comforted him with their visits. With them, he could relax and be himself. When Lisa pretended to scold him for the sorry state of his toenails, he loved it and was happy to let her cut them. He grinned when Jennifer called him "Old Man" or poked gentle fun at his uncontrollable hip swaying by nicknaming him "Elvis."

He was Dad—funny, smart, normal. He was included now in the conversation, part of their "Remember the time . . ." reminiscing about childhoods, featured in the family stories whose telling had now been turned over to the next generation. They kidded him as usual about his "genetic integrity," as Michael called it. He learned it at his mother's knee, they said, and told again the story of Marjorie's catching her five-year-old son stealing a box of doughnuts from the back of a delivery truck. She made him confess to the driver, then sweep their front porch for a penny a day, until he earned enough to repay her for the doughnuts he never got to eat. He was the only man in corporate America's history to try to turn in his frequent-flyer miles, they declared, and repeated the favorite story of Marsh's special trip to the Finance Department to pronounce that Jamesbury had paid for the flights; therefore, the miles rightfully belonged to the company. "Good Lord, Marsh," a stunned accountant had said, "there's no line item for that—what would we do with them?" And then suggested in so many words that he just go away.

Marsh was flattered that his children considered him such a paragon, but wasn't so sure himself. He spent hours with Jen, his philosopher daughter, struggling with the issue of a life well lived. Had he been a good man, he asked? He always thought he had done the right thing, but it came so easily to him, he said. Did his good deeds count if he could perform them with so little effort or personal sacrifice?

Jen tried to reassure him by explaining Aristotle's definition of happiness, which he called by the ancient Greek "eudaimonia." To Aristotle, it meant "flourishing as a human being." To reach such a state, one needed to possess a virtuous character so solid, it became natural to do the right thing. Marsh had reached this state, his daughter assured him, and its being natural for him didn't take away from the value of his acts. He could rest easy, Jennifer concluded, in an easy-to-understand two-page summary she had written, to be reread as many times as he needed. She read aloud from it now, while I stood in the kitchen and watched the role reversal as the child comforted the parent.

It was now the spring of 2006. Maybe we had always expected that 2006 would include trauma, given our pattern. Every seven years, a crisis occurred in our lives, even before we met: in 1978, Marsh's wife had left him and I had been fired from my job; in 1985, we separated for three agonizing months; in 1992, Marsh was diagnosed with cancer, in 1999, with Parkinson's. Whatever lay in wait, we could prepare ourselves by re-reading "Remember the Sweet Things," we decided. It would help us to not lose sight of the bounty we had received in our long, happy married life. No more than a few pages a day, we agreed, so we could savor them and make them last.

We sat on our porch overlooking the Pacific, and I read to Marsh from the list. It was good for me to read again the examples of uncomplicated love I had received from this dear man. Page after page, they sent me the message "You are blessed. You are one of the lucky few. Don't be so greedy as to expect more gifts than the ones you have already been given."

As for Marsh, I didn't know he was still capable of the grins that lit up his face while I read. "Let's get back to the list," he said every day, looking forward to the litany of clever remarks and good times that composed "our lovely little life." It was a melancholy morning when we ran out of pages. I expected I'd never see that look of contentment on Marsh's face again as he listened to me read about the "exemplary spouse" who delighted his wife with lettuce leaf garnishes and cooing under the covers.

A few weeks after we had shared the last page of entries, on the morning of June 3, 2006, Marsh didn't wake up. Quietly, without fanfare, he had slipped away. As if with reading the Sweet Things list, we had said our goodbyes; as if the last page signaled it was time for him to go.

I don't remember a lot about that day or the weeks that followed. I know I called Fred, a friend in San Pancho who rushed from his bed that morning to help me. Michael and our closest friends in Mexico, Priscilla and Mike, arrived within hours and stayed all that day and the next. A Mexican doctor came from the hospital in town and had me sign a form. I watched a gray hearse wind its way up the cobblestoned lane, incongruous against the backdrop of Pacific blue and jungle green. It came for my husband's body and returned the next morning with his ashes, enclosed in a wooden box and protected by the Virgin Mary's pewter likeness.

People were escorted in and picked up at the airport.

Phone calls were made and received. E-mails were read and written. Plans for a memorial service were begun. I use the passive voice because it matches the numbing calm I felt those first days and weeks. I believed the time-honored expressions of sympathy I was now receiving; Marsh and I had even kidded about them.

"Here's how funeral etiquette goes," Marsh said. "If someone says, 'It's a blessing,' you say, 'Yes, he's in a better place.'"

I continued. "And if they say, 'He's in a better place,' I say, 'Yes, it's a blessing.'"

He was in a better place and it was a blessing, for he had been spared years of indignity. He hadn't feared his own death; he had considered it thoughtfully and spoken about it openly with me and his children. What he feared, this man who loved to please, was being a burden, and from this, too, he was spared. His life had been rich in accomplishments and affection; he left with no wishes unfulfilled and no relationships in need of fixing. *Dear Marsh,* I thought, *you made a clean getaway.*

We arranged Marsh's memorial service for a month later, in the Barrington, Rhode Island, Congregational church where he had been confirmed and his children and grandchildren baptized. During that month, I worked for hours on pouches made from five of Marsh's favorite neckties. I fashioned five pouches from the pentagonal ends and a sixth pouch from pieces of each tie.

Every night, I sat in front of the droning TV, an anxious Lola leaning on my leg and never leaving my side, while I pulled cotton thread through silk fabric in the tiniest of tight stitches. I was making bags for Marsh's ashes—one bag for each of our children and one for me. They would be placed in the boxes that friend Kathy and I found in a small shop near the beach. Six handcrafted wormwood boxes with black hammered metal hinges and old-fashioned clasps and keys, perfect for "Mr. Wood."

Four weeks after Marsh died, I packed up the boxes and some clothes for the annual summer trip to the border, final destination Jennifer and Pat's house in San Jose. Lola would stay as usual with Michael and friends in Vallarta. Of my many firsts as a widow, one of the hardest was that drive alone. It wasn't the driving; Marsh hadn't taken the wheel in five years, and I could go for hours without a break. I longed for my missing sidekick. I saw him seated next to me studying a map. I pictured us listening to the radio and Garrison Keillor reading notes from members of the Prairie Home Companion audience—"To Dan, congratulations on finishing your last day of full-time employment. From your terrified dependents." I patted the empty passenger seat and said, "You'd have chuckled at that one, Marsh."

Jennifer, Michael, and I flew to the East Coast together, where we stayed with Kathy at her house in

Westborough, just a few blocks away from 29 West Street. Bill, Marsh's old friend who had skied and sailed with him for over fifty years, invited the family to his and Nancy's house for a barbecue on a balmy Friday evening before the next day's service. The people who loved Marsh most were gathered there, our mood intimate and serene, as we milled between the dock and the house, and visited in the kitchen and on the back porch.

On Saturday morning, our friends and family filled Barrington Congregational, a New England colonial classic with high-sided pews and crimson red bench cushions. Sheila and Walter arrived with an arrangement of flowers from their garden, and they placed it on the altar, just as they had done for Jennifer's wedding. We circled the flowers with the six wormwood boxes, each of which contained the pouch of Marsh's ashes and copies of his obituary, the order of service, and a tribute from Xiao Li that he had written himself and titled "Great Marsh." Xiao Li asked permission for a Shanghai carver to engrave Marsh's headstone. When he learned there would be no burial, he ordered six identical small wooden plaques, hand-calligraphed in Mandarin to read "Forever Friendship," and we affixed one to each box.

I knew the hymns Marsh wanted us to sing—we mentioned them in the will we had prepared together years ago. So we sang the Navy Hymn and "God of Grace, God of Glory," written by his uncle, Harry Emerson Fosdick. His third request was appropriate this time around. The first time had been at our wedding twenty years earlier, when Henrietta asked what he'd like to hear, then choked on her ice water and flatly refused when he suggested "I Come to the Garden Alone."

Lisa spoke first, followed by son Jeff, son-in-law Eddie, grandson Nicholas, and oldest friend Bill. Michael and our Jennifers didn't trust themselves to speak, but both daughters wrote lovely pieces for friend Dick and cousin Debbie to read. Kathy was last. She shared some of her own thoughts and then did as I had asked— she read some entries from "Remember the Sweet Things." A few were poignant, and I heard some sniffles, but most had been selected for their charm. Kathy and I picked them because they captured Marsh's style and brought him back to us. They highlighted a part of him we would never forget: the silly man rolling out wonton skins as he sang "Bringing in the Sheaves"; the thoughtful man who shoveled out his wife's car and deiced the windows; the simple man so pleased with the thickness of his grass.

When Kathy finished, we sat in silent meditation and listened to Worcester's Salisbury Singers, including bass Marshall Greene, sing Verdi's *Requiem* at Boston Symphony Hall. I had chosen the Agnus Dei, one of the few peaceful sections in the thundering work Marsh always considered his favorite. He loved to play the CD of this concert at home and join the chorus again to boom out the *Dies irae*. He would make me laugh by puffing his chest and playing to his "public" with a theatrical sweep of his arm.

That booming bass, in the dining room of 29 West, was the beloved voice I would remember.

Other voices as well.

The exhausted voice, on my front stoop, asking, "Will you have me?"

The playful voice, hopping back into bed with a cheery "Here I am again."

The frightened voice, calling from Austin with the news "It's cancer, El."

The selfless voice, saying often and from the heart, "Nothing pleases me more than doing something nice for you."

Listening to that loving voice for twenty-one years, I had known what it was to feel cherished and grounded. Now, with his voice silenced forever, I wasn't as sure of myself. Being a new widow is confusing. You are forced to join a women's club that you want no part of. You are told you look great, whether it's true or not, when you are feeling the opposite. You are called with offers of "anything we can do to help, just let us know," when you're too numb to think of what that might be. All I knew for sure was that my grieving the loss of Marsh would, in some way, go on for the rest of my life. Surely not as desperately as now, with emotions as raw. But I would never "get over" him. I would never forget what a spectacular partner he had been. I would always remember how proud I was when first introduced as "Marsh's wife, Ellen," a position I now had to give up. Lying in bed, unable to sleep, I repeated in my head what someone had quipped was a Unitarian's prayer: "I'm available. What's next?" But for me, it rang hollow. I couldn't even fathom that much optimism.

## "Remember the Sweet Things" final entry

• on January 10, 2007, my sixtieth birthday, in the middle of a dinner party in my honor, the doorbell rang. It was a delivery of a huge bouquet of dahlias, with a note reading, "Happy birthday with undying love, Marsh." Last spring he had asked Jen to remember to send them.

# Chapter 10

## *Without Marsh*

weeks after Marsh's memorial. Three pension funds, two insurance policies, name changes on accounts of all kinds—these were not unwelcome distractions. We also started work immediately on a studio apartment for me behind my daughter's house in San Jose. We called it the "Grammy flat." San Pancho would still be home, but I could spend as much or as little time in California as I wished—we would play it by ear and think of the Grammy flat as an experiment.

I started work on a piece of writing, too. My brothers, Tom and Jim, and sisters-in-law, Sally and Teri, had been moved by the Sweet Things list when they first heard about it at the service. They encouraged me to do more with it. "Write an article," said Jim, a managing editor at a major magazine. "Explain the idea of the list and how you arrived at it," he suggested, and sold me when he said, "It would make for a great tribute to Marsh."

So every day for six weeks, I sat in the quiet of the Martin Luther King Library's sixth floor and wrote. I mourned Marsh as I wrote in longhand about meeting him, about his courting me, about our years as newlyweds. The remembering had me in tears and hiding my face in my arm some days, but it was soothing, too. The writing gave me license to wallow in memories of us at our best, to dwell on the past, to delay "getting on with it" until I felt ready. For six intense weeks, I keened on paper.

I sent the piece to Jim first. He and Teri liked it, called it heartfelt, and passed it on to colleagues, who reacted the same way. Tom responded by forwarding it to the rest of the family, who gave me enthusiastic feedback. They had all liked Marsh, thought he was a great guy, and were sure he would have guffawed the loudest at the men's new inside joke:

When it comes to the ladies, ask "What would Marsh do?"

I drove back to Mexico in early September, this time with Marsh's grandson Tyler for company. The morning after arriving home in San Pancho and two weeks after sending the article to Jim, an editor from *Hallmark* magazine was on the line. Everyone in the New York office loved the piece, Helen said, and had huge crushes on Marsh. Could they feature him in their June issue the following year?

As simply as that, an incredulous, euphoric sixty-year-old would become published for the first time, and she had her husband to thank for providing the material. And I think it would have amused Marsh, the great-grandson of a valentine maker, to know that the first to be telling our story were people from the world's largest greeting card company.

I enjoyed working with Helen and other *Hallmark* staff as we edited the article over the next few months. It also helped delay the inevitable—moving out of a life as a wife and into one as a widow. It jolted me to realize that I had never lived alone; roommates, kids, and husbands had always shared my space. I tried to make light of my new status. "What a great new name—the Widow Greene," I said. "Straight out of Hawthorne; very New England." But I was lying. I loathed the word "widow." For me, it conjured up the image of a lonely woman, sitting down to a solitary cocktail at sunset and the end of another purposeless day.

Panic attacks unnerved me during the first six months after Marsh died. I would bolt out of a grocery store in Vallarta, leaving a full basket behind, desperate to get back to the security of home. Or I would excuse myself from the group at the beach or from my place at the table, unable to control the tears that came out of nowhere. Lack of energy shut me down, too, during those early months of widowhood. After an hour of conversation, the strain of pretending to enjoy myself ground me into silence, literally too sad for words.

I managed to do a few things to help myself, however. I attended meetings of the women's group some of us started four years before. I went to breakfast every Monday with other regulars in San Pancho. I met Nancy there, and teamed up with her and Gail for early-morning jungle walks; we chatted as we trudged up and down the steep dirt roads, on our way to becoming confidantes. Carolyn and I started a San Pancho writing group, and eight of us met every Wednesday to read and critique each other's work. Two of the members were published writers, and everyone had talent; we all came with new material each week, so our Wednesday sessions were productive and satisfying.

And inspiring for me. Jim was now encouraging me to expand the magazine article into a book. It seemed daunting, but the women in the San Pancho writing group guided me through my first draft and urged me on with their unabashed cheerleading.

Mostly I tried to follow Kathy's advice. A ten-year veteran of living alone, she had heard me describe myself often enough as a recluse by nature. "When invited, say yes," she said. "Don't prejudge whether you'll have a good time or not. You have to go to know. So just go."

She was right, and the practice at socializing built up my stamina for my first dinner party without Marsh. I invited Nancy and Gail, and their husbands, Skip and Bill. Defending against a case of nerves or a drop in energy, I fixed familiar, no-fail dishes I could make ahead, so dinner was ready and the table set by the time they arrived. I served Marsh's margaritas and my best guacamole as we watched the sunset on the porch. I left my guests to seat themselves at the table, while I went to the kitchen and ladled soup into six bowls. As I came back to the porch, a bowl in each hand, Skip said softly, "Ellen, I think we have one place too many." I counted the six place settings and blushed, but, among friends and longtime marrieds, I could acknowledge the tenderness of the moment. "You see, Marsh," I said, "there will always be a place at the table for you."

Our kids and some old friends came down to visit that first year alone in Mexico, and Michael and I got together regularly for dinner in Vallarta. But I needed more than a life of leisure. This was my chance to follow through on an offer I had first made in 1968 and then withdrawn. I applied again for the Peace Corps.

The Peace Corps application process is multistepped, and I made it through the forms, security clearance, personal interview in California, and physical exams. I would be considered for a teacher-training position in Central or South America; possible countries were Peru,

Bolivia, and Paraguay. I would most probably begin the twenty-seven-month assignment in September. I was excited; the prospect of returning to a classroom felt good.

But not as good as what happened in the mean-time. Andrew, a literary agent in New York City, con-tacted me in January. He had read my article, saw the same book potential that Jim had seen, and now of-fered his help in writing a proposal and finding a pub-lisher. By May, four publishers had expressed interest, and Andrew held an auction, where William Morrow bought the book. By June, he had also sold it to Italian and German publishers.

This was beyond belief. An agent? An auction? Three publishers? Something was going on here, something surreal, something beyond beginner's luck. Marsh must be in on this and pulling some strings, people kidded me. Who could resist being internationally beloved? Phone calls and e-mails flew among our family and friends as we spread the incredible news of the book sale.

The Peace Corps would have to be put on hold. I had a book to write, and obligations around promoting it. It was back to the Martin Luther King Library. Six days a week that summer of 2007, I sat in the same cubicle and wrote, pounding on a laptop this time, fleshing out the story of the life and love of Marsh and Ellen Greene.

Sometimes I talked to Marsh, there in my cubicle.

I asked him to help me get the story right, to tell the truth, to "do us proud," as we used to say to each other when one of us took off to face a challenge. I knew I ran the risk of sanctifying Marsh. Even with the Sweet Things list as proof of his dearness, I was still a new widow, pining for a man I never could see objectively. Nostalgia had probably inflated some of what I remembered, too. "Memories are like corks out of bottles," I read somewhere. "They swell. They no longer fit."

Maybe so. But then, what was the harm? My intentions were pure—by sharing the Sweet Things, I would praise Marsh and honor him. I would introduce readers to the guileless man of many talents who loved me so well, the strong man whose gentle acts softened and reshaped me into a better, less critical human being. By their example, the Sweet Things would encourage people to acknowledge the goodness in their own lives and relationships, too. To see the acknowledgment as the nurturing and attention needed in a marriage, as with anything we want to stay alive and grow.

The Sweet Things provided nurturance in death as well. The pages of line items re-created for me the treasured minutia that I might otherwise have forgotten. They were snippets of memory that gave me great comfort as I arranged them into the larger story of our life and waited for grief to transform itself into acceptance and calm.

"La vida nos esta prestada [Life is loaned to us]," the Mexicans say, and they know in their bones that the loan will be called. They recognize death, play with it, and accept it as part of the cycle of life. They destroy its morbidity by mocking it with sugar skulls and papier-mâché skeletons, burying it with music and remembrances on the Day of the Dead. Last year my grief had been too raw to celebrate with them; by November 1, 2007, I would be ready.

On our porch, I would shape three boxes into a pyramid and cover it with a white cloth, making an altar with a view of the sea. On it I would place a picture of Marsh—my favorite, on *St. Kilda,* barefoot and smiling—and nestle tea candles in seashells we collected on countless walks down long-forgotten beaches. I would surround him with nosegays of marigolds and arrays of favorite foods—a plate of stuffed mussels, of course, and a bowl of garlic soup; a handful of oatmeal cookies and a sprinkling of pistachio nuts—in hopes that the smells would entice his return to take part in the remembrance. When the sun set that evening, I would play Verdi's *Requiem,* as sung by the Salisbury Singers. I would light the candles, pull up a chair, and read aloud from the Sweet Things, inviting Marsh home for a joyful reunion as I kept vigil through the night.

# Some Thoughts on Creating a List of Your Own

I HAVE BEEN ASKED TO GIVE GUIDANCE ON writing your own Sweet Things list and must admit to the resistance I feel. It seems preachy and presumptuous of me, as someone unqualified personally or professionally to give advice.

I worry, too, about anyone starting a list because he or she sees it as a solution to a seriously unhealthy relationship. Keeping a list is not going to convert a partner into a better person, nor should it justify a person's bad behavior toward you. I would go so far as to say that keeping a list probably won't change an abusive person one bit.

I wasn't trying to turn any ship around. I had a good thing going from the beginning with Marsh; all I had to do was observe and share. All I can say now is that my keeping this list has been helpful to me, and it might be helpful to you, too.

## *Where to begin*

I see my list as mainly noticing small gestures and re-cording short statements. You look for them and you write them down—on sticky notes; in your day planner; on your cell phone or BlackBerry. Everything, you write down everything, not waiting for grand gifts and co-medic jewels. You can edit later, and throw things out. What did s/he say that made you smile? What did s/he do that made you say "thanks"?

What if nothing about this person makes you smile or gives you cause for thanks? Perhaps further reflec-tion would break up the logjam. What first attracted you to this person? What is s/he doing now that rein-forces those things, that maybe you've grown to take forgranted? How did you describe this person to your mother whom you wanted to impress? What does s/he do and say now that shows s/he's still that same person?

Here are a few examples of what I mean. Let's say you are a woman who was attracted to your husband-to-be because he was good with kids. What does he do now, as the father of his own? Does he read to them, for instance? Okay, you might jot down

- "read to Sarah while putting her to bed"

But you can do better than that if you observe more closely. What if he

• "read *Bears in the Night* to Sarah for the twentieth night in a row"

Or how about

• "entertained himself, reading *Bears in the Night* to Sarah for the twentieth night in a row, in a New Jersey mobster accent"

Let's say you described him as a considerate man who could be counted on to help around the house. You might watch him outside on a pleasant autumn day and duly note

• "raked up the leaves in the backyard"

But he probably wouldn't glow after reading that about himself. If you watched a bit closer, you might be able to milk it for more

• "his methodical way of raking up leaves every fall, shaping them into equal-sized piles six feet apart"

Or maybe a double mention if the methodical raker then undoes his hard work to give his daughter a good time

• "forming a giant pile of leaves and calling for Sarah, who squeals with delight as she jumps on top and sends the leaves flying"

### How much to write

I suppose the length of your entries depends on how much you like to write. Even then, as someone who enjoys writing, I kept mine short—usually just a sentence or two. I was after quantity, for starters. And if I had made the list keeping into labor-intensive storytelling, I doubt if I would have kept it up. Plus it might have reflected too much of me, the writer, when the goal was to focus on Marsh, the subject.

Longer entries were often pieces of dialogue that needed to be included in their entirety. Sometimes I would group snippets into a paragraph, too. For example, I combined a dozen or so remembrances into one paragraph that began "the Christmas holidays at Quinta Elena:" Another began with "traveling down the coast of the Pacific Northwest."

A word on voice. I chose to use the third person "he" and "his," as if I were writing to another person and not to Marsh. As I explained at the beginning of the book, I might have had a divorce attorney in mind. I guess when I changed the motivation from negative to positive, I didn't change the voice. You could just as easily speak directly to the subject and use "you" and "your."

## Whom to focus on

The obvious subject of a list is your partner in romance. But other candidates come to mind as well. I wish I had kept a list on my teenagers, for example. They were hilarious then; they still are now. It would be so much fun now to reread all the high school antics and snappy remarks.

Or start even earlier. We stop the baby books after recording the first words. We should keep the book going, and jot down those precocious childhood turns of phrase and voyages of discovery. Jennifer recorded this anecdote from six-year-old Anna, announcing at dinner that a girl in her first grade class had been stung by a bee: "But justice came swiftly," said Anna, "for the bee was smooshed with a big fat book."

Or this explanation from three-year-old Lily, standing on a chair in front of my Christmas crèche, fondling a figurine: "This guy is Jesus' dad. His name is Joe."

I could have improved a relationship with my mother, too, by keeping a list and sharing it with her. She needed more words of appreciation than I probably gave. And it would be meaningful to me to have a written record of her at our best.

## *How to share it*

There's magic in volume, I think. Acknowledging a thoughtful gesture at the time is, of course, the thing to do. But reading about it months later, along with many others, reinforces how special the person is to you.

So I put a year's worth of entries in a Valentine's Day card. They could just as well have been tied to a bottle of champagne, sent as an e-mail, or read in person or over the phone.

You might choose to go with a different day. It could be your wedding anniversary or during your annual vacation. It could be twice a year, too, if you have enough entries, or simply pulled out when you need them to get over a bad patch.

There are countless options for a list. It could be a once-a-year gift on birthdays, religious holidays, Mother's Day, or Father's Day. It could be a once-in-a-lifetime gift for loved ones when they graduate, get married, or have babies. A list could also be maintained as an ongoing historical record, with the hope of its being passed down to next generations, almost always eager to know the up close and personal story of the people in their family.

# Acknowledgments

THE IDEA FOR THIS BOOK CAME DURING MARSH'S memorial service. Jim Herre and Teri Thompson, my brother and sister-in-law, listened to the reading from the Sweet Things list and recognized the potential. Because of their insight, urging, and help, this book exists, and I thank them.

The book began as an article read by Rob Fleder and Marilyn Johnson, who forwarded it to Helen Rogan at *Hallmark* magazine. I thank Rob and Marilyn for their support, Helen for her artful editing, and all the *Hallmark* people for their elegant treatment of the material and personal warmth with me.

It is my good fortune to have Andrew Stuart for an agent. A believer in this book project from its inception, he gave me confidence as he guided me through the procedures for writing and selling a book. Andrew is thoughtful and thorough, and I trust his judgment without question.

Evidence of Andrew's good judgment was his sending the proposal to Sarah Durand at William Morrow. With impeccable taste, Sarah showed me how to flesh out our story and make it a richer experience for readers. She and assistant Emily Krump found ways to improve the manuscript with hands so light, the process was a pleasure from beginning to end. Thanks, also, to Jennifer Pooley as she saw the book through to publication.

This book has been in good hands at William Morrow. Lisa Gallagher was its champion from the onset and has overseen it every step of the way. Sonia Greenbaum cleaned up the copy and made me look good. Lynn Grady, Tavia Kowalchuk, and Brianne Halverson marketed it with clever promotional ideas. Joyce Wong shepherded it through the production process. My sincerest thanks to all of them for helping the book be all that it can be.

I thank Bill Polleys, Kevin Rose, and Marilyn Hague who answered my myriad requests for clarification and details. I am grateful to Kathy Welcome, Priscilla Herzoff, and the San Pancho Writers'—Nancy Brown, Gail Mitchell, Carolyn Kingson, and Channing Enders— all of whom read first drafts with affection and a keen eye. Their enthusiasm has been boundless, their input invaluable. Most of all, I cherish their friendship.

My brother and sister-in-law, Tom and Sally Herre, could not have been more encouraging. The same goes for Marsh's and my children: Michael Garcia, Jennifer Garcia-Daly, Lisa Painter, Jeff Greene, and Jennifer Greene are as excited as I am that readers will get to know the man we loved and miss so much. And who is the person, finally, to whom I owe the most heartfelt thanks. Thank you, Marsh, for all of the Sweet Things that inspired this book, a book that for me is a last, long love letter to you.

# Endpaper Photo Captions

Marsh with his first grandchild, Tyler Whitney Greene, in 1984.

Marsh and Ellen kissing at their wedding.

Marsh on the *St. Kilda*, 1989.

The *St. Kilda*, 1989.

Marsh.

Marsh with his business partner Xiao Li.

Marsh and Ellen biking, Christmas card, 1992.

Family Christmas gathering, 1992.

Marsh and Ellen.

Marsh and Nen on her wedding day.

Lola and Michael.

Marsh and Lola in the cactus garden.

Marsh with Anna and Lily on our beach.

Marsh's seventieth birthday.

Marsh and Ellen, 2003.

Marsh and Ellen in the Scottish Highlands.

Marsh and his three adult children.

Fresh tracks.